THE BEST OF

Soul

THE BEST OF

Soul

The Essential CD Guide

Ralph Tee

CollinsPublishersSanFrancisco
A Division of HarperCollins*Publishers*

First published in the United States in 1993 by Collins Publishers San Francisco,
1160 Battery Street, San Francisco, California 94111

Library of Congress Cataloging-in-Publication Data

Tee, Ralph.
    The best of soul : the essential CD guide / Ralph Tee.
       p. cm. — (The Essential CD guides)
    Discography: p.
    Includes index.
    ISBN 0-00-255340-6
    1. Soul musicians—Biography—Dictionaries. 2. Soul music—
History and criticism. 3. Compact discs—Reviews. I. Title. II. Series.
ML102.S65142 1993
781.644—dc20   93-11545
                                           CIP
                                           MN

Printed in Great Britain

THE AUTHOR

Ralph Tee is an acknowledged expert on soul music and former
Assistant Editor of *Blues & Soul* (UK) magazine. He is a senior executive for
Skratch Records and is the author of *Who's Who in Soul Music* published
by St. Martin's Press in 1991.

Contents

INTRODUCTION

* * *

*T*HE STORY OF SOUL IS ONE WHICH COMMENCED THE BEST PART OF 40 YEARS AGO, AND ONE WHICH INCORPORATES SINGERS, SONGWRITERS, MUSICIANS AND PRODUCERS WHO HAVE HAD AN IMMEASURABLE IMPACT ON POPULAR MUSIC.

This book traces the origins of people and places synonymous with soul music from its roots through to the present day. Naturally it would be impossible to include everybody who has made a contribution to soul music over the years—there have been thousands who have either written a classic song or recorded a blissful 45—but I believe this compendium reflects all that is truly significant and all that is relevant to today's CD buyer.

The Best of Soul takes a close look at 100 soul stars and a closer look at 10 soul legends who over the years have shaped soul music into what it is today. While there are considerably more artists than the 110 this book has room for, I have made my choice based on each artist's individual album chart success, and the availability of each artist's albums on the CD format. As vinyl becomes increasingly more scarce, CD is the way ahead.

The listings section included in this book catalogues every album by all 110 artists that has charted either in the UK (Top 100) or USA (Top 50) over the years, and is available on CD. Where the album has not been made available on CD in the UK, an American CD catalogue number has been listed (where possible) . In the case of albums released on CD neither in the UK nor the USA, a Japanese catalogue number has been listed (again where possible). In the case of albums issued in the UK on CD, but deleted, the deleted number will appear, and where chart albums by major artists have not been issued on CD anywhere at all, compilation CDs featuring tracks from such albums have where possible been included.

The artist profiles combine factual information with my own feelings for those who have given me so much personal pleasure over the years, particularly vocalists. Soul music boasts some of the finest, most talented and individual voices in any music idiom. In what other form of music would you find the diversity and uniqueness of singers like Aretha Franklin, Chaka Khan, Otis Redding, Marvin Gaye, Randy Crawford, Gladys Knight, Deniece Williams,

Minnie Riperton, Roberta Flack, Sam Cooke, Linda Jones and Mica Paris? There simply is no other!

Where it has not been possible to include an individual artist profile, due to space and the lack of album chart activity rather than critical acclaim or single pop hits, I have endeavoured to include them in the Story of Soul section of the book which deals with the various different areas of soul which have been particularly significant over the years.

In the case of artists from the late Fifties and Sixties, it should be noted that albums were generally compilations of singles, and some artists didn't get to release albums at all.

It was only from the late Sixties that singles were released in conjunction with albums—and from the Seventies that singles were released as a means of promoting albums (as in commercial terms more money is to be made from albums than from singles).

While in more recent times the UK has played more of an active role in soul music—it has only been from the late Eighties that artists like Mica Paris, Lisa Stansfield, Soul II Soul, Loose Ends, Caron Wheeler, Chris Ballin, Act Of Faith, Omar, etc. have emerged—it is the mighty USA where the roots of soul music lie, and which continues to nurture the finest talent.

Historically it has been cities like Detroit ("The Motown Sound"), Philadelphia ("The Philly Sound/ Disco"), New York ("Atlantic/ Disco/Hip Hop"), Memphis ("Stax"), Los Angeles ("Warner Bros/United Artists"), and Chicago ("Curtom/ Chi-Sound") where soul music's finest moments have been created, and it is cities like these, together with their studios, producers, musicians and singers, that are looked at in this book.

Possibly the hardest decision I had to make in putting the book together was choosing just 20 albums to highlight for either their outstanding contribution to soul music, or their significance in terms of either innovation or commercial success. It was particularly difficult because I was unable to include so many of the albums I have personally treasured over the years.

As well as establishing household names, soul music has been responsible for many generations of fanatics, each with its own idea of what a truly great soul record really is, and each with its own collection of special singers and songs that miss the commercial spotlight. All such treasures, however, stem from the legacy of talent and outstanding achievements left by the major league talent that is traced through these pages.

There are also many outstanding new artists who have come through too recently to be included here. Artists like Rachelle Ferrell, Gary Taylor, Hari Paris, Chris Ballin, Victor Haynes and Nikita Germaine, who will secure a new generation of soul.

There are also many session singers or artists on small labels who could not be included as they never enjoyed major chart success.

RALPH TEE

DETROIT and the MOTOWN SOUND

The Sound of Young America

*W*HEN MOTOWN RECORDS AND MANY OF ITS MAJOR ARTISTS QUIT DETROIT IN THE EARLY SEVENTIES FOR THE UNDOUBTED BUSINESS OPPORTUNITY ATTRACTIONS OF THE WEST COAST, IT WAS SAID THAT THE HEART WAS RIPPED OUT OF THE CITY WHICH HAD GIVEN THE COMPANY ITS UNIQUE AND WORLD-CHANGING SOUND.

Certainly, while other Detroit operations like Westbound soldiered on, things were never quite the same again in the grimy but vibrant northern industrial city and, while the phenomenal success of Michael Jackson and others took Motown to a new level of success, so too the instantly recognizable musical identity on which earlier triumphs had been built became irreparably dissipated. The new-look Motown admittedly made far more money but, effectively, it became just another label.

It would be a mistake, however, to assume that Motown was Detroit, for long before Berry Gordy and his sister Anna first launched their innovative company, a string of major artists—starting with the blues giant John Lee Hooker and including such worthies as Eddie Floyd,

Wilson Pickett and Aretha Franklin—had elevated themselves from the Detroit ghetto projects to international stardom.

It was, indeed, the songwriting royalties from Jackie Wilson's 1957 hit 'Reet Petite' and recordings by Marv Johnson for United Artists which had in the first place given Gordy the funding with which to quit his job on the automobile production line and become a full-time record producer.

Motown began operations in June 1960, its first release being 'My Beloved'/'Sugar Daddy' by doo-wop quintet the Satintones. The sister Tamla label followed a month later and soon there were Gordy, Soul, and other labels too.

Barrett Strong's 'Money', later covered by the Beatles, was an early smash hit but it was a couple of years before the oh-so-distinctive Motown sound crystallized with the Miracles' million-selling 'Shop

The Supremes reflected the spirit of Detroit's Motown Records in the Sixties and later launched a solo career for Diana Ross.

Around' and the Marvelettes' chart-topping 'Please Mr Postman'. That was when the floodgates truly opened and the "Hitsville USA" nameplate

Berry Gordy, now retired from Motown.

tagged on the company's West Grand Boulevard headquarters—a couple of modest converted houses in a residential district of Detroit—became truly justified.

Usually driven by Benny Benjamin's hot-shot drumming and James Jamerson's pulsing bass lines, plus great horn arrangements, Earl Van Dyke's piano or organ and percussion which often included tambourines and cowbells, and a string section moonlighting from the local symphony orchestra, Motown became, in its own words, "the sound of young America".

The corporation created its own stars, grooming such artists as Marvin Gaye, Diana Ross And The Supremes, Martha And The Vandellas,

Smokey Robinson And The Miracles, the Velvelettes, the Four Tops, the Temptations and many others not just in studio techniques but, through a special dance school, in stage presentation too.

By the mid-Sixties, already established artists like the Isley Brothers and Gladys Knight And The Pips were being attracted to the roster—even Tom Jones came close to signing—and the discovery of the Jackson Five found the Motown sound totally shaking off the shackles of the black ghetto and becoming music for kids everywhere.

It was no surprise to find the company launching the Rare Earth label to showcase the white psychedelic soul rockers of the same name and the addition of Norman Whitfield and other new-wave producers to the already well established Holland, Dozier and Holland triumvirate saw the Motown sound move into a new dimension with the freaky synthesized arrangements increasingly employed on records by the Temptations, Undisputed Truth and other acts.

When upcoming local companies like Golden World and Ric-Tic seemed set to challenge Motown's dominance of the Detroit scene, Gordy and his right-hand man Barney Ales took the simple expedient of buying them and their artists' contracts—which is how Edwin Starr, for instance, came into the fold. That said, Holland, Dozier and Holland did manage to break loose and establish their own highly successful Invictus label.

Marvin Gaye's epic *What's Going On* album and Stevie Wonder's *Innervisions* set represented a watershed, these two stars managing to wrest artistic control away from the company. Other acts like the Isley Brothers, who set up their own label, and Gladys Knight And The Pips won their freedom by actually leaving the fold.

Michael Jackson owes much of his success to his guidance from Detroit's Motown Records.

By that time, Motown had already moved out of the ghetto into plush downtown offices and, with eyes on broader horizons, the subsequent move to Los Angeles was perhaps inevitable. Motown's profits soared but the Sound of Detroit had passed into history.

THAT MEMPHIS BEAT

Stax of Soul

Tina Turner with husband Ike at the start of their career in Memphis.

*S*TANDING BESIDE THE MIGHTY MISSISSIPPI, MEMPHIS HAS LONG BEEN ONE OF AMERICA'S GREAT CROSSROADS CITIES. IT IS NO SURPRISE, THEN, THAT IT HAS PLAYED SUCH A MAJOR ROLE IN THE EVOLUTION OF AMERICAN POPULAR MUSIC.

The city which was birthplace to W. C. Handy—self proclaimed "Father of the Blues"—and which gave the world the talents of Elvis Presley, Jerry Lee Lewis, Roy Orbison, Carl Perkins and other originators of rock 'n' roll, was also a fountainhead of soul music.

Ike Turner arrived in the city from Clarksdale, Mississippi, and found early work discovering blues artists like B. B. King and Howlin' Wolf for West Coast and northern labels, Rufus Thomas worked as a local DJ before becoming the father figure of the Memphis soul movement, and Willie Mitchell's hard-driving combo confidently crossed the divide between R&B and soul music. So, too, did such mighty talents as Bobby "Blue" Bland, O. V. Wright and the tragic Johnny Ace—who died on Christmas Eve 1954, blowing his brains out in a senseless game of Russian roulette when poised to become probably the first soul superstar.

It was from this rich musical environment that Stax Records received its nourishment. A spin-off of the Satellite record shop, the label started modestly enough with records by Rufus Thomas and his daughter Carla, found early national success with the Mar-Keys' 'Last Night' and Booker T And The MGs' 'Green Onions' and quickly defined the raw, earthy "Memphis Beat" sound which was to become such a major force in black American music through the Sixties and early Seventies.

Sam And Dave, William Bell, Eddie Floyd, the Mad Lads and, most importantly of all, Otis Redding, defined a sound which provided the most formidable challenge to the until then all-conquering dominance of Motown. Gospel

Isaac Hayes was more than just "Shaft"; he was
instrumental in numerous Stax triumphs.

act, the Staple Singers used the
Stax sound to win secular success,
while bluesman Albert King
employed it to broaden his appeal.
Moreover, New York-based Atlantic,
which distributed Stax for the first
decade, sent many of its own
artists—including Wilson Pickett
and Don Covay—down to the
Memphis company to record.

The Stax studio on East
McLemore Avenue soon became so
busy that the studio band role played
by Booker T And The MGs, as
rhythm section, and the Mar-Keys
(later renamed the Memphis Horns)
as brass section, developed into a
near round-the-clock shift system
with the younger Barkays outfit. Otis
Redding's death in an air crash on
December 10, 1967, along with all
but two of the Barkays (one who had
missed the flight and the other the
sole survivor of the accident),
marked the end of an era.

Label founder Jim Stewart and
Estelle Axton sold out to the massive Gulf + Western organization

and Isaac Hayes emerged from his role as a producer, session musician and general factotum to become a gold-bedecked soul superstar. Stax reached new heights with the Wattstax and Soul II Soul concerts and movies—but the bubble was about to burst. Stewart and his A&R chief, former DJ Al Bell, bought the company back but over-extended themselves financially and Stax collapsed in 1975, leading the bankruptcy hearing judge to make the wry comment: "It seems to me that running a record company is akin to playing Russian roulette—with five bullets in the chamber!"

The rival Hi label, which had gradually been growing in status across town with the developing careers of Al Green, Ann Peebles, Syl Johnson and Otis Clay, among others, took over where Stax left off, Willie Mitchell's tighter than tight combo providing a similar sock-it-to-me gutbucket soul framework. Hi was not the only challenger.

Goldwax had its moments too—especially with the superlative recordings of James Carr. Nor should the more soulful contributions of blue-eyed outfit the Box Tops, on Bell Records, be overlooked.

The story of the Memphis Beat belongs not only to these stars but equally to such backroom talents as Chips Moman, Dan Penn, Spooner Oldham, Al Jackson Jr., Steve Cropper, Donald "Duck" Dunn, Andrew Love, Wayne Jackson, the Hodges brothers, Howard "Tiny" Grimes and all the other great producers, songwriters and backing musicians.

With Goldwax and Hi having both followed Stax into oblivion, Memphis today lacks a musical focus. The city still abounds with talent however, and locals will tell you the Memphis Beat is far from dead—it's just taking a short and well-earned respite.

With his group Soul II Soul, Jazzy B helped to gain the respect of UK soul in America.

BIG APPLE SOUND

The Sound of New York

*A*s AMERICA'S MOST POPULOUS METROPOLIS AND MAJOR TRADING CENTRE, IT IS NO SURPRISE TO FIND NEW YORK PLAYING SUCH AN IMPORTANT ROLE IN THE EVOLUTION OF SOUL MUSIC— NOR TO FIND THAT, GIVEN SO MANY DIVERSE ELEMENTS COMING INTO AND PASSING THROUGH THE CITY, IT HAS NEVER ESTABLISHED AN ALL-EMBRACING SOUND OF ITS OWN, AS HAPPENED WITH DETROIT, MEMPHIS AND PHILADELPHIA.

The legendary Apollo Theatre in Harlem continues to make or break soul music legends.

Small and unprepossessing as it might have been, Harlem's Apollo Theatre was undoubtedly the most prestigious venue of all for black acts over many decades—both established stars and hopeful newcomers. Its infamous amateur nights have passed into legend, with unforgiving audiences likely to pelt unimpressive performers, and stagehands waiting in the wings to hook the no-hopers off the stage with a long pole.

But if you conquered the Apollo crowd and won their hearts, then the world of black music was your oyster. It was here that many of the great acts-to-be earned their first recording contracts and, naturally, the local New York-based labels were first in line to pick up those valuable signatures. In the early days, there were soul pioneers like Ruth Brown and LaVern Baker; later on Dionne Warwick, Chuck Jackson and many others had their hour of glory. And if they couldn't cut it on stage, then there was always session work to be had at the Big Apple's numerous recording studios—a line of apprenticeship followed by many eventually big acts when they were first starting out.

From the famed Brill Building (the original "tin-pan alley") on Broadway came a steady flow of great songs from talented writers, white and black alike. Leiber and Stoller (with the Coasters and the Drifters), Jerry Goffin and Carole King (with Little Eva), Burt Bacharach and Hal David (with Dionne Warwick and Chuck Jackson), Bert Berns (first with Atlantic acts then with his own

Shout label roster)—all came up with hit after hit after hit.

There were plenty of labels too: Rama, Gee, Roulette, Gone/End, Apollo, Savoy, Old Town, Red Bird, Roulette, Sue, and Jubilee were all vying for talent. Most successful of them all, right through to present times, has been Atlantic.

Started in 1947 by Nesuhi and Ahmet Ertegun, the jazz-loving sons of the Turkish ambassador to Washington, and their Jewish American partner Herb Abramson, Atlantic had its finger on the pulse right from day one—despite undertaking the formidable task of covering the whole gamut of black music from modern jazz to rural blues, from doo-wop to soul. Early successes came with the Drifters, initially led by Clyde McPhatter, and the novelty songs of the Coasters—and then came the phenomenal success of Ray Charles, regarded by many as having been, along with Sam Cooke, the spiritual father of the soul genre and an inspirational source.

Abramson's share in the company was eventually bought out for a

Dionne Warwick, indebted to New Yorkers Bacharach And David.

then princely $300,000 by Jerry Wexler, who was to prove to be one of soul music's most successful producers through his brilliant work with the likes of Wilson Pickett, Don Covay, Solomon Burke and Aretha Franklin. It was Wexler's inspired idea to ship his biggest artists out to record at Stax in Memphis, Fame in Muscle Shoals and, later on, to Sigma Sound in Philadelphia—though Atlantic's own New York studios had been prodigiously successful, using such redoubtable talents as sax

The Drifters helped to shape the sound of soul music in New York during the Sixties.

Atlantic's closest challenger in the Sixties hey-day of New York soul was Florence Greenberg's Scepter/Wand stable of labels, where Luther Dixon was house producer. As at Atlantic, every effort was made to create a family atmosphere and it worked well, bringing major success to Dionne Warwick, Chuck Jackson, Tommy Hunt, Maxine Brown, the Shirelles and others.

While Dionne Warwick had the largest measure of commercial success, the big-voiced Chuck Jackson—a singer on whom Tom Jones based his style—was arguably the company's greatest talent, cutting a steady succession of classic sides over a 10-year period. When he finally quit to sign for Motown, Chuck seemed destined for even bigger things but, unfortunately, Detroit was unable to replicate the magic he had found in New York.

Today, New York continues as a musical melting pot, attention now switched to the hip-hop music of the Bronx and Queens projects.

genius King Curtis, guitarists Eric Gale and Cornell Dupree and bass player Jerry Jemmott to create a wholly distinctive sound.

Though now part of the vast Warners conglomerate, Atlantic has managed to preserve much of its independence and remains a black music force to this day, supporting the richest back catalogue in the business with contemporary signings like En Vogue, Levert and Intro.

THE PHILLY SOUND

The Sound of Philadelphia

*A*MERICA'S SELF-PROCLAIMED "CITY OF BROTHERLY LOVE", PHILADELPHIA HAS A PROUD MUSICAL HERITAGE. IT WAS IN PHILLY THAT BESSIE SMITH, "THE EMPRESS OF THE BLUES", BASED HERSELF; THE CITY FOSTERED THE TALENTS OF CHARLIE PARKER, THE CREATOR OF BE-BOP, WHEN HE BLEW INTO TOWN FROM KANSAS CITY, AND WAS HOME TO THE REVERED JAZZ ORGANIST SCHOOL WHICH INCLUDED JIMMY SMITH, JIMMY McGRIFF, BROTHER JACK McDUFF AND RICHARD "GROOVE" HOLMES.

Dick Clarke's trend-setting *American Bandstand* TV pop show was beamed from the city, exploiting such local rock 'n' roll talents as Bobby Rydell, Frankie Avalon, Fabian, Steve Alaimo and Chubby Checker and, right from soul's early days, the city made an important contribution.

Labels like Cameo Parker (with the Orlons, Bunny Sigler and others), Artic (with Barbara Mason), Showtime (with the Showstoppers), Jamie-Guyden and Swan were all based there while local DJ Jimmy Bishop became one of America's most important black music promoters with his lavish package shows, first at the Uptown Theatre and later in the

city's massive football stadium. In 1968, the Delfonics gave us their sound of sexy soul with the sophisticated 'La La Means I Love You' and 'Ready Or Not, Here I Come' and Thom Bell moved on from masterminding their pioneering sound to engineering the Stylistics' phenomenal rise to stardom.

Great though Bell's contribution to the

Teddy Pendergrass was one of Philadelphia's most prolific vocalists of the Seventies.

Philly Sound might have been, it was overshadowed by the work of his close friends Kenny Gamble and Leon Huff whose Philadelphia International label took over in the Seventies from where Motown left off. The Intruders, the O'Jays, Harold Melvin And The Bluenotes (from which group Teddy Pendergrass emerged to find solo stardom), Archie Bell And The Drells, Billy Paul, the Three Degrees, the Jones Girls, People's Choice and other Philadelphia International acts became cogs in a relentless hit machine. The company revived the careers of such already established talents as Lou Rawls and Jerry Butler.

Other labels sent artists like Joe Simon, Johnny Mathis, Dionne Warwick, Wilson Pickett and Aretha Franklin into town to pick up on some of the magic—and it worked, with each of them enjoying "Made in Philadelphia" hits. Numbers like Billy Paul's 'Me And Mrs Jones', Harold Melvin's 'The Love I Lost' and

The Three Degrees summed up the Philly sound on MFSB's 'TSOP' (The Sound Of Philadelphia).

'If You Don't Know Me By Now', the Intruders' 'I'll Always Love My Mama', Lou Rawls' 'Lady Love', Teddy Pendergrass's 'The Whole Town's Laughing At Me', MFSB's 'TSOP', the Three Degrees' 'When Will I See You Again' and 'Year Of Decision' and Archie Bell's 'Dance Your Troubles Away' all have solid claims to being recognized among the all-time classics of soul music.

Working in their lavishly equipped Sigma Sound Studio and using such songwriting talents as Carry Gilbert, Victor Casterphen and McFadden And Whitehead to supplement their own output, Gamble and Huff had the sure touch of gold. The sound they created was fresh, thoroughly modern and highly sophisticated, replete with complex orchestral arrangements and using a studio big band led by Dexter Wansell and known as MFSB (which usually stood for "Mother, Father, Sister, Brother" or "Mother F***ing Son of a Bitch", depending on who you asked). Perfect for its time, this remarkable music has proved itself to possess superb staying power, sounding as contemporary today as it did when it was first issued to an adoring public.

Turned into artists, McFadden And Whitehead contributed the smash hit 'Ain't No Stoppin' Us Now' as 1979's biggest dance club favourite and it seemed a prophetic title at the time. However, the loss of key acts to other labels, and the bad car smash which sidelined Teddy Pendergrass for several years and left him partially crippled, saw the Philadelphia International magic crumble and the company slipped into a steady decline which led to virtual inactivity by the end of the Eighties, though recent times have seen Kenny Gamble and Leon Huff making major steps to get their act back together.

CALIFORNIA SOUL

The Sound of the West Coast

"California here we come!" was a clarion call for many black Americans during the Second World War years when the busy shipyards and aircraft factories of the West Coast offered plenty of work and the promise of a better life than that to be had sharecropping in the fear-filled Deep South, where segregation reigned and the Ku-Klux-Klan was on the rampage.

With a welter of incoming musical influences, the recording studios of Los Angeles, Oakland and San Francisco were able to offer a rich kaleidoscope of sounds and, with young blacks rapidly turning away from the rough, raw sounds of rural blues in the search for something more sophisticated, the seeds were sown for the emergence of a vibrant soul scene. Indeed, Ray Charles, working first out of Cleveland then later in LA, and Sam Cooke, also in LA, have been widely credited as the two most important figures in reworking gospel stylings to create a whole new art form under the soul banner, Ray maintaining a recording career through to this day.

They were not alone, of course. Showcased within the Johnny Otis Revue the very young Esther Phillips and Etta James were making their own contribution and the plethora of West Coast "bird groups" were transforming doo-wop into early soul group stylings, while the Coasters were flitting between LA and New York laying down some of the best goodtime R&B sounds ever—

Ray Charles was instrumental in carving secular soul from gospel traditions.

'Yakkety yak, don't talk back!' Majors like Capitol, United Artists, Warner Brothers and MGM as well as independents—among them Aladdin, Kent/Modern, Flair, Specialty and Imperial/Minit—were thirsty for new talent. There seemed to be an unending supply.

Ike Turner, with wife Tina in tow, arrived in this milieu via St Louis and New York to quickly establish their Bolic Sounds Studio and commence a bewildering blur of album releases which cropped up on a host of different labels before the dynamic duo finally arrived on the major United Artists label.

The eccentric and enigmatic Phil Spector, besides producing Ike and Tina Turner's 'River Deep, Mountain High' classic—banning Ike from the studio in the process—was defining his "Wall of Sound", turning out the most expensive single in history with the Checkmates Limited cover of Creedence Clearwater Revival's 'Proud Mary', for which no fewer than 900 musicians were

hired and fired before he was satisfied with the end result.

Bob and Earl gave us the dance-floor anthem 'Harlem Shuffle' but were firmly rooted in Los Angeles. Under his pseudonym of Jackie Lee, Earl Nelson, who had served his apprenticeship with the Hollywood Flames, gave us a repeat dosage with 'The Duck', a truly silly song—but what a stormer—as well as writing Love Unlimited's début hit 'Walking In The Rain'. The producer of that effort was one Barry White, who through the Seventies brought a new perspective to what seductive soul balladry was all about.

Bob Relf, Earl Nelson and Barry White all worked prolifically with Mirwood, an ambitious little label which set out to establish its own distinctive sound after the pattern set so successfully elsewhere by the likes of Stax and Motown. Meanwhile, Bill Withers, who started his working life fitting toilets to jumbo jets in the Boeing factory, had

Barry White symbolized Seventies soul with its lavish productions and international success.

21

Sly Stone illuminated the West Coast's music scene with his innovative fusion of funk and rock.

the mid Seventies to early Eighties saw the establishment of Dick Griffey's highly successful Solar (Sound of Los Angeles Records) label and the rise of dance-floor queens Donna Summer, Carrie Lucas and Sylvester(!). Pose was all, and Griffey summed up the new rules when he said: "If I sign an artist, I expect him to sound like Donny Hathaway, write like Stevie Wonder, dance like Fred Astaire and look like Adonis!" Inevitably, he signed few artists that fitted this demanding bill, but the label still carries on successfully.

revealed himself as a unique singing and guitar-playing talent.

Then along came flower power, psychedelia and progressive rock,and the West Coast black music scene redefined itself through the power-house sound of Tower Of Power and Larry Graham and the freaky output of Sly And The Family Stone.

The arrival on the Coast of the Motown corporation provided fresh impetus and the disco explosion of

THE WINDY CITY SOUND

The Sound of Chicago

*F*EW CITIES IN THE WORLD CAN CLAIM A MUSIC SCENE AS VIBRANT AS THAT WHICH THRIVES IN CHICAGO, "THE WINDY CITY". THE BEST OF IT WAS BROUGHT TO THE BUSTLING LAKESIDE METROPOLIS AS A VALUABLE BY-PRODUCT OF THE GREAT BLACK MIGRATIONS FROM THE DEEP SOUTH DURING THE THIRTIES AND FORTIES.

Known as the world capital of the blues, Chicago evolved its unique and vibrantly exciting form of that music from sounds which had originated from the Mississippi Delta country. Check the biographies of most of the city's many soul music stars and you will find their roots were in gospel singing in southern churches.

Given such a rich vein of talent on hand to be tapped, Chicago has always been well served with recording outlets. In the pre Second World War era, major record companies like RCA (with Bluebird) and Columbia (with OKeh) set up specialist "race" labels to cut records by blues artists. They astutely located these specialist operations in Chicago where there was a proven ready market for the product. In more recent times landmark companies like Brunswick, Mercury, Vee Jay and Chess have also made their home base in the city—though often bringing in artists from out of town to bolster their locally-based rosters. Brunswick thus signed Jackie Wilson (and also, through Dakar, gave us Tyrone Davis); Mercury shipped in Brook Benton to work alongside locally-based Dinah Washington; and Chess recorded Washington's Billy "Fat Boy" Stewart as well as Maurice and Mac and Etta James, who resided locally.

Among the groups which were born in the Chicago projects, the Chi-Lites were the stand out act. They first appeared on Vee Jay as the Chanteurs before devising a new name which paid tribute to their roots. Driven by the cool falsetto of Marshall Thompson and utilizing to the full the redoubtable songwriting talents of group member Eugene Record, the group enjoyed more

With 'Have You Seen Her', the Chi-Lites epitomize the sound of Chicago.

Social commentator, Curtis Mayfield used soul music as a medium for his beliefs.

than two decades at the top, thanks to such classics as 'Give More Power To The People', 'Have You Seen Her', 'Homely Girl', 'I Found Sunshine' and 'Too Good To Be Forgotten'.

Chicago's other key vocal act was the Impressions, who originated from out of town. Sam Gooden and Fred Cash, from a Chatanooga, Tennessee group called the Roosters, had arrived in Chicago independently, met up again and teamed with Jerry Butler, who had moved from the South years earlier as a 3-year-old, and then with 14-year-old locally-born Curtis Mayfield in 1958 to form the Impressions and score with 'For Your Precious Love'.

That mega-hit led Jerry Butler into a highly successful solo career and, for a while, Curtis Mayfield joined him as songwriter and guitarist. In 1961 he rejoined the Impressions for a solid run of hits on ABC Paramount which perfectly showcased his pure falsetto lead vocals. 'It's Alright', 'Keep On Pushing', 'People Get Ready', 'We're a Winner' and by now on Curtis's own Curtom label, founded in 1968, the socially conscious 'This Is My Country', 'Choice Of Colours' and 'Mighty Mighty, Spade And Whitey' gems led to Curtis's illustrious solo career, which commenced in 1970 and reached a peak with the *Superfly* soundtrack album.

Tragically, Curtis was victim of a freak on-stage accident at a charity event in New York, when a lighting rig fell on him and left him paralysed from the neck down.

Today the Chicago baton has been taken up by the house and hip-hop bands which abound in the teeming and run-down inner-city ghettos. In fact house music takes its name from the warehouses (and bath houses come to that) where DJs like Frankie Knuckles created the house scene from the ashes of disco. Combining technology with DJ skills and a relentless disco beat, Chicago became the centre of the house music scene from where labels like DJ International and Trax created international hits for artists like Farley "Jackmaster" Funk and Darryl Pandy, and DJs like Steve "Silk" Hurley, who went on to work with a cross-section of soul artists from Kym Sims to Michael Jackson.

Chicago, in fact, dominated the house music scene of the mid-Eighties. Ultimately this led to a less soulful dance scene and the start of the techno scene which had everything to do with dancefloor adrenalin, but nothing to do with songs

One of Chicago's most important groups, the Impressions launched careers for Jerry Butler, Leroy Hutson and Curtom Records founder Curtis Mayfield.

or soul vocals. As more and more white people became the backbone of this music, the less black people could relate to it. The result was that the hip-hop scene broadened to incorporate soulful vocalists, and artists like Mary J. Blige marked the time of a new era in soul music whereby black artists made black music and kept it for themselves. To date, white folk have yet to get fully to grips with the urban form of ghetto soul.

FUNKY BUSINESS

The Sound of the Drum and Bass

*A*s ONE WOULD EXPECT OF SOMETHING CREATED FROM SUCH A WIDE DIVERSITY OF DIFFERENT INFLUENCES, SOUL MUSIC IS A WONDERFULLY KALEIDOSCOPIC MUSIC FORM, MOVING IN MANY DIRECTIONS AT THE SAME TIME AND OVERLAPPING WITH SUCH OTHER STYLES AS BLUES, JAZZ, COUNTRY, ROCK 'N' ROLL AND POP.

When the mood gets low-down and raunchy, then the word "funk" springs to mind but that definition, like the definition of soul itself, means many different things to different people. What we can be assured of is that funky music, whatever direction it comes from, aims straight at the gut and the feet—its appeal is essentially rhythmic rather than melodic and the lyrics are often merely repetitive phrases rather than the poetic artistry found in, for example, deep soul.

The term "funk" originated in the world of jazz and was appended to the music produced by artists like Cannonball Adderley, Johnny Hammond, Jimmy Smith and Jimmy McGriff, who added a large dab of R&B flavouring to their particular slant of jazz.

Confusingly, funk/jazz was very different from the very similarly titled but far more calculated and clinical jazz-funk style which emerged in the mid to late Seventies. This latter style was aimed very much at the disco dance floor and reached its zenith in the work of talents like Roy Ayers, the Crusaders, Stanley Clarke, Herbie Hancock and Ronnie Laws—though a great deal of dross was marketed under the same tag.

In other areas, funk verged towards rock music via the high-volume, near-psychedelic stylings of Sly And The Family Stone, Graham Central Station, the Blackbyrds and the Chamber Brothers. The master of this particular idiom has surely been the colourful George Clinton with his various acts including Parliament, Funkadelic and the Brides Of Funkenstein. George worked regularly with Bootsy Collins who had first emerged as a core member of James Brown's backing band the JBs, a seminal outfit led by Maceo Parker, Pee Wee Ellis and Fred Wesley.

If any one man could claim to be the father of funk it was Soul Brother Number One himself, the peerless James Brown—who was not slow to dub himself "the King of the new new Super-Heavy

George Clinton pioneered his own brand of P-funk with groups like Parliament and Funkadelic.

Funk". With its thudding beat and swirling rhythms, gut-wrenching horn work and chunky guitar playing overlaying the fatback beat of bass and drums which were tighter than tight, James Brown's funk set dance floors alight, right from the days of 'I Feel Good' and 'Papa's Got A Brand New Bag' through the golden era of 'Sex Machine' to the brand new album *Universal James*.

We shouldn't forget, though, that the word "funk" was appended just as strongly to the flood of dance records which emanated from the Stax studios in Memphis during the Seventies and early Eighties. While other soul styles have been regionally dominated, from the Motown sound of Detroit to the smooth uptown soul harmonies of New York and Philadelphia, funk has permeated black America at every level and has inspired UK music too.

Through the late Eighties, the term "funk" became largely unfashionable as "house", "garage" and "techno" dance idioms grabbed the spotlight on dance floors. In fact "rare groove" became a more popular term for older funk records which maintained modern-day interest, although today "funk" is a term slowly creeping back in to define, for some, the hip-hop and swing beat dance records of today—"swing beat" being a Nineties equivalent of Seventies funk, but with electronic rather than acoustic-orientated productions. The term is used less today than in the Seventies, but remains a legitimate definition in contemporary black music.

THE ROOTS of SOUL

The Early Days

"*What Is Soul?*" Ben E. King asked in the opening line of a Sixties hit and promptly gave the simple but at the same time profound answer "Soul is something from deep inside". More an emotion than a science, soul is an enigmatic nebulous musical idiom which originally evolved from an amalgam of uninhibited gospel stylings and secular blues themes.

Dig into the background of most great soul artists and you will find they started out singing in church and, to this day, the gospel influence is all pervasive. Yet there are other strong strands too. Indeed, it was within jazz that the term "soul" was first used, while the crossover influence from white country music has been considerable, especially at the ballad end of the spectrum. Take the better samples of Nashville songwriting, add a solid fatback backing and a great soul voice and you have some of the most potent soul music of all. Candi Staton's electrifying version of Tammi Wynette's 'Stand By Your Man' and Bettye Swann's emotion-drenched reading of Hank Cochran's 'Don't You ever Get Tired (Of Hurting Me)?' are true classics, while Ray Charles's 1952 *Modern Sounds In Country And Western* set was a landmark in the early development of soul with its mighty 'I Can't Stop Loving You' and other memorable tracks.

Along with the late, great Sam Cooke, Ray Charles is popularly credited with having been the spiritual father of soul music and there is no doubt he was an enormous influence on the likes of James Brown and Bobby Bland, just as Sam Cooke inspired Otis Redding, Arthur Conley and many others. However, soul's roots go back much further than the output of these two worthy artists, while earlier R&B influences like Roy Brown, Roy Milton and Louis Jordan also played a part in defining the soul style which almost spontaneously burst into being as the rocking Fifties turned into the to the swinging Sixties.

Regional idioms too played a major role in soul's evolution. Down in New Orleans, the rich tones of Fats Domino's singing and the piano- and sax-dominated nature of his backing tracks provided inspiration for a whole school of soul artists, starting with Chris Kenner and Ernie K. Doe and continuing with Lee Dorsey and Betty Harris, while the distinctive sounds of Memphis, Chicago, Philadelphia and Detroit

Candi Staton had hits in the Seventies, but was one of the pioneers of soul music in earlier years.

each tipped a hat towards an earlier rich local heritage of blues music.

Yet it has been the world of gospel music, more than any other style, which has wielded the greatest influence over the way in which soul music has become the musical life-force of modern black America. The relationship between the sacred and the profane has not always been an easy one. Artists like Sam Coke, Johnnie Taylor, Aretha Franklin, the Womacks and many others faced great opprobrium when—in the view of gospel purists—they sold their souls to tin-pan alley. Today such prejudices have largely disappeared, allowing the Staple Singers, for one example, not only to switch between the two idioms but to blur the dividing edges into essentially modern soul.

Soul has also crossed over so much with both rock and pop music that pigeonholed definitions become almost meaningless, for how can you accurately catagorize the music of Sly And The Family Stone, the Chamber Brothers, George Clinton and many others than with the single, simple

The music of Fats Domino inspired a whole new generation of soul artists.

word "good"? It's just not that easy. It is a continuing two-way street, the highly successful *The Commitments* movie—set in Dublin—fluently illustrating just how great an influence soul music has become throughout the world.

Motown once described itself as "the Sound of Young America". It might be said that soul music has become "the Sound of the Young", whichever country they happen to come from.

BEYOND COUNTRY

The Sound of the South

$\mathcal{T}$HOUGH MANY ARTISTS SUBSEQUENTLY MOVED NORTH OR WEST TO FIND FAME AND FORTUNE IN THE MAJOR CITIES OF PHILADELPHIA, DETROIT, CHICAGO AND LOS ANGELES, THERE IS NO QUESTION THAT THE DEEP SOUTH HAS BEEN THE GREAT SPAWNING GROUND FOR SOUL MUSIC TALENT AND THAT THE CHURCH HAS BEEN ITS NURSERY.

Though better known as the world capital of country music, Nashville, Tennessee, has also made a major impact in soul circles, thanks to such artists as Joe Simon, Peggy Scott and Jo Jo Benson, and white singer Timi Yoro, whose sides cut in the southern city were on a par with the finest work of her two greatest influences, Dinah Washington and Little Esther Phillips (who cut her own finest sides in Nashville).

Atlanta has made its contribution too, and is now home to Ichiban, the highly active company owned by Englishman John Abbey who, through his pioneering *Blues And Soul* magazine did so much to establish a strong soul music following in the UK during the Sixties and Seventies. Among the soul acts signed to Ichiban are such highly respected veterans as Ben E. King, Jerry Butler, Clarence Carter, William Bell and Tyrone Davis.

Atlanta is also home to the contemporary soul sounds of writers/producers L.A. and Babyface, their LaFace label (via Arista) being home to such artists as T.L.C. and the *Boomerang* sound track from which came the biggest selling R&B single of all time 'End Of The Road' by Boyz II Men.

Down in Houston, Texas, Don Robey's Peacock Club was for many years a magnet to black talent, leading him to start Peacock Records, one of the most important gospel outlets, and to acquire the Duke label, founded by Memphis DJ James Mathis.

Through Duke and its Backbeat offshoot, Robey fostered the careers of such major stars as Johnny Ace, Bobby "Blue" Bland and O. V. Wright. Bobby Bland now records for Malaco, an Alabama-based label which has developed its own distinctive sound and become a repository for such long established artists as Little Milton and Johnny Taylor, as well as having discovered people like Dorothy Moore and disco heroine Fern Kinney.

Alabama is also home state to Candi Staton, a remarkable talent who, along with Bettye Swann and others defined what deep soul is all about, often taking country music songs and adapting them blacker than black—her version of Tammy

Wynette's 'Stand By Your Man' being a masterpiece of its type. Like her former husband Clarence Carter, Candi recorded many of her best sides in the Muscle Shoals, Alabama, Fame Studios owned by Rick Hall and whose session crew—including such formidable talents as Roger Hawkins, Barry Beckett, David Hood, Gene "Bowlegs" Miller and rock guitarist Duane Allman—rivalled that of Stax over the state line in Memphis, Tennessee.

We should not forget that it was in the South—Augusta, Georgia, to be precise—which first gave us the raw funk and emotion-laden ballads of James Brown and his Famous Flames prior to his funk era.

Golden-voiced Percy Sledge cut his memorable 'When A Man Loves A Woman' in the backroom of a Sheffield, Alabama, record shop owned by Quin Ivy, the Jewel/Paula/Ronn set-up worked out of Louisiana and, at the peak of the Seventies disco boom, the Miami, Florida-based TK group of labels emerged as a force with such artists as George and Gwen McCrae, KC And The Sunshine Band, Latimore, Betty Wright (who was licensed to Atlantic), and a host of wide-ranging talents covering everything from raw funk to bland disco.

But if any city challenged Memphis as the major southern centre for soul music, it was surely New Orleans. Having already given us the best work of Fats Domino, Little Richard, Lloyd Price and Larry Williams, the Crescent City ushered in the soul sale with goodies by such artists as Robert Parker, Irma Thomas, Ernie K. Doe, Chris Kenner, Jessie Hill, Lee Dorsey, the Meters, the Neville Brothers and many others.

The catalyst for much of the best was that remarkable songwriter, pianist, singer and producer Allen Toussaint, who also made some very fine records of his own. Working out of his Seesaint Studio, and using the Meters as house band, Allen and his partner Marshall Sehorn largely defined the distinctive keyboards and horn-driven New Orleans sound.

Throughout the South to this day, in the big cities and sleepy country towns, there's a host of independently owned recording studios each fervently hoping to discover the next great talent. Just as the soul brothers and sisters of the Sixties usurped the blues artists of previous times, so today it is the sound of rap. But one thing is for certain, through all the changes, the richest vein of new black music talent runs below the Mason–Dixon line.

Percy Sledge defied the disco boom with 'When A Man Loves A Woman'.

BLUE-EYED SOUL

The Role of White People in Soul Music

*W*HILE SOUL MUSIC IS ESSENTIALLY A BLACK AMERICAN PHENOMENON, THE ENORMOUS ROLE PLAYED IN ITS DEVELOPMENT BY WHITE PEOPLE, ON BOTH SIDES OF THE ATLANTIC, SHOULD NOT BE OVERLOOKED.

Black American audiences expressed their tacit approval of blue-eyed soul artists like the Righteous Brothers (and more recently George Michael) by putting their records in the R&B charts, while in Britain artists like the incredibly talented Georgie Fame, Zoot Money and even the Beatles helped spread the soul creed. Tom Jones, Dusty Springfield and Cilla Black plagiarized the music remorselessly but, if nothing else, helped interest white middle-class audiences in the black ghetto music of Motown and Stax.

However, the most important role played by white people in the development of soul music took place behind the scenes. For starters, most of the record companies were owned by white business people and where, as in the case of the Berry Gordy-owned Motown operation, blacks were able to take their commercial destiny in their own hands, they called on white help and experience in helping them compete effectively with the major labels.

The role Barney Ales played as Gordy's right-hand man was crucial to Motown's success, just as Jerry Wexler helped his Turkish partners Nesuhi and Ahmet Ertegun to make such a success of Atlantic Records. In the case

Booker T's Steve Cropper and Duck Dunn defined the Stax sound.

of Kenny Gamble and Leon Huff's Philadelphia International label, it was Clive Davis who signed the operation to CBS and instigated PIR's funding prior to launching Arista and being behind the careers of Aretha Franklin, Dionne Warwick and Whitney Houston through to this day.

Right from the early days of soul, white session men were used regularly and in many cases not merely followed but helped set the course of the music. Steve Cropper and Duck Dunn within Booker T And The MGs defined the Memphis soul sound of Stax, with Cropper's sparse yet so perfect style—which said more in three notes than most players could in a dozen—winning the universal respect of his black musical contemporaries.

The Muscle Shoals sound was essentially forged by white musicians and session players around the country who might otherwise have been languishing on country music sessions, yet found a new passion to

capture their interest and nourish their creativity thanks to Stax.

The honour roll of blue-eyed contributors to soul is long and distinguished: Phil Spector with his famed "Wall of Sound" which brought stardom to the Crystals and the Ronettes and helped Ike And Tina Turner to their classic 'River Deep, Mountain High'; Joe South's incisive guitar work on so many of Aretha Franklin's best records; the production work and session playing of Dan Penn and Spooner Oldham; Mac "Dr. John" Rebennack's work with so many of the best New Orleans artists.

White songwriters too have made a very real contribution. Some have worked almost exclusively within the soul idiom, others have found their songs being freely borrowed by black artists. Pop and especially country music songbooks have provided a rich hunting-ground. The Rolling Stones and the Beatles might have filled their early albums with cover versions of records originally made by such soul artists as Marvin Gaye, Arthur Alexander, the Miracles and the Isley Brothers, but the debt was more than repaid. Otis Redding covered the Stones' 'Satisfaction', Ike And Tina Turner scored with their version of the Lennon/McCartney 'Get Back', and Stevie Wonder—an artist much covered by white recording artists—cut 'Yesterday' among other pop songs.

As for country, well that music has proved perfect for adaptation—the great blues singer/guitarist B. B. King, a huge fan of the Nashville idiom, having once explained it all by saying "country is white man's blues music". Artists like Joe Simon, Percy Sledge and Bettye Swann largely built their careers on giving soulful interpretations of country material before winning recognition as soul singers.

The role of white audiences has also been crucial, providing a level of record sales which black consumers alone could never have sustained. In Britain, soul music became the clarion call of the hippest kids on the block. No self-respecting Sixties mod was fully dressed without a copy of the latest soul import album tucked under his arm, while in later years the northern soul, disco, and jazz-funk movements provided a continued happy hunting-ground for black America's great gift to world culture and entertainment which continues through to today.

ADEVA

Adeva is the first R&B/dance music singer of the present generation, but has not as yet achieved the status of such pioneering women-singer predecessors as Grace Jones or Annie Lennox. What success she has had to date can definitely be attributed to her assertive persona and gospel-rooted vocals, although it must be admitted that her voice does not rank among the greats.

The name "Adeva" comes from "diva", meaning a strong-voiced female singer. Born in New Jersey, she began her singing career in local clubs while working professionally during the day as a school teacher. When the Easy Street label in New York released her début single 'In An' Out Of My Life' in 1988, singing took over from teaching as her priority.

Her main success so far has been in the UK, where Cooltempo Records have released such hit dance songs as 'Respect', 'Warning', 'Musical Freedom', 'Beautiful Love' and 'Treat Me Right' from an album *Adeva!* Having signed worldwide to Capitol records in 1992, Adeva's career is bound to take off in new directions.

STEVE ARRINGTON

Steve Arrington was the distinctive voice of funk group Slave in their heyday, 'Just A Touch Of Love' (1979) being the group's only hit, although they recorded a legacy of great music. Born in Ohio, Steve originally played drums with the group and then sang backgrounds before taking over as lead singer in 1978 and leaving his mark on songs such as 'Watching You', 'Wait For Me', and the aforementioned hit.

Steve left Slave in 1983 after some internal wrangles and formed his own group, Steve Arrington's Hall Of Fame. They made a début recording in 1984 with an album *Positive People* for Atlantic Records, but Steve went solo the following year and scored the biggest hit in his career with 'Feel So Real' from an album *Dancin' In The Key Of Life*.

In 1986 Steve "discovered God" and became a born-again Christian which took his focus away from music. With the exception of a one-off recording for Manhattan/EMI, he has not recorded since.

ASHFORD AND SIMPSON

Husband and wife duo Ashford And Simpson are one of the few writing and performing partnerships who have lasted the test of time in a great soul tradition. They are best known as songwriters and producers with an impressive portfolio of artists, in particular Marvin Gaye and Diana Ross. On all levels they are clearly well suited and inspired, if perhaps individually they have not and are unlikely to be able to match the great depth of creative output they've achieved over the past two decades as a team.

Adeva is a legitimate soul singer for the Nineties, but still awaits recognition beyond the dance scene.

Nick Ashford (born in Fairfield, South Carolina, in 1942) and Valerie Simpson (born in New York in 1946) first met in Harlem's White Rock Baptist Church, and from 1967 worked at Motown with Marvin Gaye And Tammi Terrell ('Ain't Nothing Like The Real Thing'/'Ain't No Mountain High Enough'), and Diana Ross, whose solo career they nurtured with songs 'Reach Out And Touch (Somebody's Hand)', 'Remember Me' and 'The Boss'.

Their production style involves lush banks of strings, crisp horns and tight rhythm sections laden with bright piano and melodic bass lines, utilized on their own hit record 'It Seems To Hang On' (1978), but not so much on their biggest hit 'Solid'.

From 'Ain't Nothing Like The Real Thing' in the Sixties to 'I'm Every Woman' in the Nineties, Ashford And Simpson are one of soul music's most prolific songwriting duos.

ATLANTIC STARR

Atlantic Starr made the most sophisticated of modern soul ballads and classiest of dance tracks over a 10-year reign from the late Seventies. The nucleus of the band are brothers David (vocals/keyboards/guitar), Jonathan (keyboards/trombone), and Wayne Lewis (vocals/keyboards). Over the years they have featured outstanding female singers, but none have yet gone on to great things as solo artists. The brothers, however, have adapted their slick productions successfully to other groups like the Mac Band.

Formed in Los Angeles, Joseph Phillips (percussion), Koran Daniels (sax), Clifford Archer (bass), William Suddeeth III (trumpet), Porter Carroll Jr. (drums/vocals) and originally Sharon Bryant (vocals) became Atlantic Starr, who first cultivated their sound with producer James Anthony Carmichael on some glorious songs, including 'When Love Calls', 'Circles', 'Love Me Down' and 'Touch A Four Leaf Clover'.

Barbara Weathers took over when the group reduced its members to Wayne, David, Jonathan and Joseph and began producing themselves in a new style which relied less on big budget orchestrations and more on sophisticated synthesizer arrangements, scoring success with 'Secret Lovers', 'Silver Shadow' and 'Always'.

PATTI AUSTIN

Patti has been greatly aided in her career by her godfather Quincy Jones and has a great deal of artistic recognition in jazz as well as soul mediums. She comes from the traditional school of jazz artists and, like other great jazz singers, she has mastered the art of conveying songs in a mature and adult way rather than having a unique vocal ability.

Born in New York in 1948, Patti became a top session singer before commencing a solo career with CTI records, although it was Quincy Jones who brought her major recognition on his award-winning platinum album *The Dude* on songs 'Betcha Wouldn't Hurt Me', 'Somethin' Special', 'Razzamatazz' and 'Turn On The Action' (1981). When Quincy Jones launched his Qwest label, Patti became his first signing. She has since enjoyed success, particularly on duets with James Ingram ('Baby Come

To Me'), Michael Jackson ('It's The Falling In Love'), and George Benson ('Moody's Mood For Love').

PHILIP BAILEY

The lead falsetto vocals of Philip Bailey graced an impressive run of hits for Earth Wind And Fire from the early Seventies to the mid-Eighties, and while he continues to work with the group through to this day, it is primarily a solo career in gospel music he pursues these days. He is one of the lasting and truly great falsetto voices known in soul music, possessing the unique ability to open up on a level more common in female artists and stir the more sensitive side less commonly found in men. He has not had the same level of success as a solo artist, but has established such a hard-core following that he will always continue to further the legacy of classic soul music.

He was born in Denver in 1951 and joined Earth Wind And Fire at the age of 20 as both vocalist and percussionist. His solo career commenced in 1983 and his most successful solo album was *Chinese Wall* (1985) which featured 'Easy Lover', the duet with Phil Collins

ANITA BAKER

Anita was heralded as the voice of the Eighties in soul circles, and few could argue that she was one of the few major artists to emerge during this decade who had a truly unique voice to combine with some of the best songwriting and productions of that time. Deservedly, she commanded the respect as one of the truly great soul singers of all time, although the promise and potential of her initial works have yet to be matched. Specializing more in the jazz genre, she has become more of a stylist rather than a great expressionist in the true soul tradition.

Born in Memphis in 1957 and raised in Detroit, her first record company said she couldn't sing. In the late Seventies she was a featured lead singer with a local group Chapter 8, but after one self-titled album for Ariola (1979) they were fired by the label.

The Beverly Glen label gave her an opportunity to record a solo album in 1983 and, with a host of top musicians and producers, *The Songstress* was released to high acclaim. However it was her *Rapture* album for Elektra which pushed Anita into the major league and established Chapter 8 guitarist Michael Powell as a major new writer and producer.

* * *

* * *

REGINA BELLE

Regina Belle has been compared at times with Anita Baker, and it is true that she launched her professional career shortly after Anita's major breakthrough and with the help of Anita's producer Michael Powell. In actual fact, while their vocal styles are similar, Regina suffers from the comparison, and the fact that she does not possess the degree of uniqueness necessary to bring her through into the league of the recognized masters, excellent though she may be. She has, however, been more diverse in her musical expression, approaching broader areas of dance music and MOR, though this may not necessarily have been to her advantage.

Regina was born and raised in New Jersey. She was discovered by a New York DJ who instigated a recording session with the Manhattans on a song 'Where Did We Go Wrong' in 1986, prior to her solo career with Columbia Records since 1987.

GEORGE BENSON

George Benson is one of the few jazz artists who has successfully conquered both the soul and pop music markets while still maintaining a loyal jazz following. Being an excellent singer as well as a talented songwriter, musician, performer and interpreter, he became the most successful artist among those who took advantage of the close

George Benson came from jazz roots as a guitarist and became an international star as a soul singer with songs like 'Give Me The Night'.

links between jazz-funk, soul and crossover pop that existed briefly from the late Seventies to the early Eighties.

Born in Pittsburgh, Pennsylvania, in 1944, he first played professionally alongside Jack McDuff before the CTI label signed him as a session guitarist, and eventually a solo artist in 1971. For the next five years he established a reputation for himself on the American jazz scene before changing labels to Warner Brothers and making the transition in 1976 from an earthy funk style to a mellow, richly orchestrated sound.

From here his vocals took prominence on hits 'Nature Boy', 'Love Ballad', 'Give Me The Night', 'Love X Love', 'Turn Your Love Around', 'Never Give Up On A Good Thing' and others.

BOOKER T AND THE MGS

Booker T. Jones and his group of session musicians the MGs created the "Stax Sound" of the Sixties and worked as the house band for the Stax label alongside their work as a group in their own right. Their sound encompassed country/blues piano chords, establishing the B-3 Hammond organ style through the Sixties.

Born in Memphis in 1944, Booker formed the MGs (standing for Memphis Group) in 1962. It consisted of Steve Cropper (guitar), Donald "Duck" Dunn (bass), Al Jackson (drums)—shot dead in 1972—and Booker himself (keyboards, also songwriter/producer). Their music at Stax was utilized by artists including Otis Redding, Eddie Floyd, Judy Clay, Sam And Dave, William Bell, Albert King and Rufus Thomas, while as Booker T And The MGs they enjoyed US chart success with singles 'Green Onions' (1962), 'Chinese Checkers' (1963), 'Outrage' (1965), 'Hip Hug Her' (1967) and 'Soul Limbo' (1968), the latter hit being their UK Top 30 chart début.

In 1968 the group disbanded, although in the UK they notched up three further hits in 1969 with 'Time Is Tight' from the movie *Uptight*, 'Soul Clap '69' and an issue of their US chart début 'Green Onions'.

BOYZ II MEN

In the US Boyz II Men have now sold over 4 million copies of their début album *Cooleyhighharmony*. It is claimed to be the country's biggest selling R&B album ever, a statement which, while controversial (officially Michael Jackson, Janet Jackson, Prince, etc. are considered "pop acts"), marks a considerable achievement for the group's four vocalists Nathan "Alex

Boyz II Men echo traditions of the Fifties in the Nineties.

Vanderpool" Morris, Michael "Bass" McCary, Wanya "Squirt" Morris, and Shawn "Slim" Stockman from Philadelphia (who formed the group in 1988).

Vocally, their recordings echo the tradition of Fifties and Sixties doo-wop groups, interweaving the sweetest of harmonies with gospel-drenched powerful lead vocals, although to date no one member has proved himself as being of the same calibre as Ruffin or Kendricks.

They are, however, important in the history of soul music in that they are the first to come out of the vocal tradition of the Temptations and the Four Tops, apply the Nineties R&B production idiom known as new jack swing, and cross the result over to a big pop audience.

JOHNNY BRISTOL

The voice of Johnny Bristol will be familiar to soul fans from the 1974 classic 'Hang On In There Baby', but his career as a songwriter, producer and recording artist spans from the Sixties through to the present day.

Born in Morganton, North Carolina, Johnny began his recording career in Detroit singing duets with Jackey Beavers. Among these early recordings was their version of Johnny's song 'Someday We'll Be Together', later a hit record for Diana Ross And The Supremes (which Johnny produced).

Through the mid-Sixties he was husband to Iris Gordy, sister to Motown founder Berry Gordy, and often with partner Harvey Fuqua wrote and produced at the Motown label for artists including Junior. Walker And The All Stars ('How Sweet It Is', 'What Does It Take'), Diana Ross, Marvin Gaye And Tammi Terrell, Smokey Robinson, David Ruffin, Edwin Starr, Michael Jackson ('25 Miles'), Gladys Knight And The Pips ('I Don't Want To Do Wrong', 'Help Me Make It Through The Night'), Martha Reeves ('No One There'), Jimmy Ruffin, the Detroit Spinners, the Four Tops and Stevie Wonder ('Yester-Me, Yester-You, Yesterday').

He also had solo hits with 'Love Me For A Reason' (his composition which became a hit for the Osmonds), and 'Love No Longer Has A Hold On Me'.

BROTHERS JOHNSON

The Brothers Johnson have been on the perimeters of the black music scene as writers and musicians since the early Seventies, while their own recording success is notable for their one dance-floor anthem 'Stomp', and a jazz-funk classic 'Streetwave'.

Brothers George (guitar/vocals, born 1953) and Louis Johnson (bass/vocals, born 1955) first played together with Billy Preston before Quincy Jones hired them as session musicians for his *Mellow Madness* album and ended up using four of their songs.

In 1976 Quincy produced their début album *Look Out For No. 1* and worked closely with them on their bass-laden orchestrated funk on classics 'Get The Funk Out Ma Face', 'I'll Be Good To You', 'Strawberry Letter #23', 'Ain't We Funkin' Now', and 'Ride-O-Rocket'.

During the early Eighties they produced their own albums and took on solo careers before a reunion album in 1988, although their next great success was on the Quincy Jones album *Back On The Block* which featured their song 'I'll Be Good To You' (with vocalists Chaka Khan and Ray Charles).

BOBBY BROWN

One of black music's most successful recording artists of the Nineties, Bobby already has three solo platinum albums to his name and a string of hit singles that epitomize contemporary urban funk known as swing beat or new jack swing. Of the crop of modern day black male singers, he epitomizes the credentials necessary to become highly successful in modern music, more so for his overall attributes rather than simply his voice.

Bobby was born in Boston in 1969 and was a former member and lead singer of the teen R&B group New Edition, which scored three platinum albums with *New Edition* (1984), *All For Love* (1986) and *Heart Break* (1988) and launched careers for fellow members Ralph Tresvant and Bell Biv Devoe.

In 1986 Bobby launched his solo career with a début album *King Of Stage*, although it was only when he teamed up with producers (and key of the swing beat sound alongside Teddy Riley) L.A. and Babyface on a second album *Don't Be Cruel* (1988) that his career took off with the songs 'My Prerogative', 'Every Little Step', 'Roni', and 'Rock Wit' Cha'.

JAMES BROWN

See separate entry in the Legends section.

Now married to Whitney Houston, Bobby Brown coupled contemporary urban black rhythms with a "bad boy" image to become internationally famous.

PEABO BRYSON

Since the late Seventies, Peabo Bryson has established himself as one of America's finest balladeers, and while in the UK his albums haven't reached the gold status of his American releases, he is generally recognized for some outstanding duets and a handful of "rare grooves" on the two-step soul scene. He has always had relative recognition and respect for his classic soul singing style, but has never reached the heights of some of his fellow artists.

Born Robert Peabo Bryson in Greenville, South Carolina in 1951, Peabo signed to Capitol Records in 1978 and enjoyed a successful run of albums for the label, although in the UK he went generally unnoticed until he teamed up with Roberta Flack for an album of duets *Born To Love* (1983) from which 'Tonight I Celebrate My Love' gave him his only major UK hit.

CAMEO

Cameo evolved from the mid Seventies as a regular funk band to be the instigators of an ultra-slick techno funk group in the mid-Eighties. Originally a 13-piece conglomerate formed in New York by Larry Blackmon, the group first recorded as the Players and made their début single 'Find My Way' in 1976.

As Cameo they attached themselves to the burgeoning funk scene in the US, and while in the UK they

Reduced to a trio in the Eighties, Cameo were one of the few funk bands of the Seventies who lasted into the new decade.

attained somewhat of a cult status through the Seventies, record sales were nowhere near their series of gold-selling albums back home. Having moved to Atlanta, Georgia, in 1982, the group underwent a dramatic change and trimmed down to four members Larry Blackmon (lead vocals/drums), Tomi Jenkins (vocals), Nathan Leftenant (trumpet), and Charlie Singleton (guitar).

Fusing Seventies funk with Eighties technology the group created a brand new sound which, for the first time, encompassed a commercial appeal with its melodies and productions that both kicked on the dance-floor and were radio-friendly. From here came their most successful commercial period with songs like 'She's Strange', 'Single Life', 'Attack Me With Your Love' and 'Word Up'.

CHANGE

Change was the brainchild of French entrepreneur Jacques Fred Pétrus and was put together with French musicians in New York in 1980. While making their first album they engaged the services of lead singer Luther Vandross who, before establishing his own solo career, gave the group three single hits with 'The Glow Of Love' (the title track from the album), 'A Lovers' Holiday' and 'Searching'.

Following this initial success an official line-up for the group was organized, James Robinson stepping in as lead singer for their début concert tour and subsequent albums *Miracles* (1981) and *Sharing Your Love* (1982).

When Rick Brenna and Debra Cooper took over as joint lead vocalists for the group in 1984, Change became a vehicle for up-and-coming songwriters/producers Jimmy Jam and Terry Lewis to prove themselves, and they excelled with an album *Change Of Heart* which, with both the title song and 'You Are My Melody', typified the popular urban black sound of the mid-Eighties and made Jam and Lewis the hottest R&B production team of the day.

Change made one more album, *Turn On Your Radio* (1985), but have not recorded since the fatal shooting of Jacques Fred Pétrus a few years later.

THE CHI-LITES

The Chi-Lites were originally Eugene Record, Marshall Thompson, Robert "Squirrel" Lester, and Creadel "Red" Jones, a vocal group who derived their style from fellow Chicago groups the Impressions and the Dells in the Sixties, but enjoyed their heyday in the Seventies with some extremely well-crafted songs.

Under the direction of local entrepreneur and producer Carl Davis, the Chi-Lites hit the big time with their first million-seller 'Give More Power To The People' in 1971, and from then enjoyed their most prolific period with a string of hits including 'Have You Seen Her'. This success showcased the warming, if perhaps indistinctive, tenor vocals of their lead singer Eugene Record, and brought particular attention to his immense songwriting skills (some of the best through the Seventies).

CHIC

Chic evolved out of the halcyon days of disco, and for a time cornered the market with an innovative sound that used strings almost percussively rather than orchestrally, which had become the norm in this music idiom.

These earthy-sounding strings combined with a special blend of rolling bass and picky guitar became the basis of the Chic sound, which was disco at its most credible with songs that have survived the test of time. Chic are recognized as being one of the most successful pop crossover black groups of this late Seventies era, and it could be said that, in the same way that Abba were great exponents of Euro pop disco, Chic were of black pop disco—although they haven't had any great success since that period, even though they reformed only recently.

The nucleus of Chic were Bernard Edwards (bass) and Nile Rodgers (guitar), who first tested the waters with 'Dance Dance Dance (Yowsah Yowsah Yowsah)' in 1977, following which the group was officially formed with the addition of drummer Tony Thompson, and joint vocalists Alfa Anderson and Luci Martin. From here they entered their most successful period with a string of hits including 'Everybody Dance', 'Le Freak', and 'Good Times', while their production sound was later utilized by Sister Sledge and Diana Ross.

NATALIE COLE

Natalie Cole is one of the few artists ever to have achieved anywhere near the same recognition and star status as one of their parents. Her musical repertoire has spanned the classic songs of her father's era right through to the commercial dance music of her time and, although never achieving the hallmarks of her father or other great female singers, she is very well respected.

Maybe not the legend her father is or even the most accomplished vocalist, but Natalie shares similar respect and success.

Born in Los Angeles in 1950, Natalie is the daughter of the legendary Nat King Cole, but after making her stage début at the age of 11 alongside her father, it was Taj Mahal who greatly inspired her during her university days to make singing her career.

Natalie combined what she had learned from the traditional form of tailor-made soul so superbly performed by her father with broader styles in jazz, folk and rock. She worked with writers/producers Chuck Jackson and Marvin Yancy (her first husband) on a succession of gold and platinum albums for Capitol Records from 1976, and by the late Eighties crossed over successfully to mainstream pop.

and the whole world began slow dancing to their records.

The original line-up was Lionel Richie (lead singer), William King (guitar/keyboards/trumpet), Walter "Clyde" Orange (drums/keyboards/vocals), Milan Williams (guitar/keyboards/vocals), Ronald LaPread (bass) and Thomas McClary (guitar/vocals) who met at college and began playing professionally in New York City. Initially a support act for the Jackson Five, the group were ultimately signed by Motown at a time when the label was embracing changes towards big production funk and moving away from the traditional "Motown sound" they had cultivated in Detroit in the Sixties. They had just one notable success with 'Night Shift' following Richie's departure.

THE COMMODORES

The Commodores were one of the most successful soul groups of the Seventies, charted 12 albums in 10 years and made a superstar of their lead singer Lionel Richie. The group, attired in flares and afros, started out in Tuskegee, Alabama, in 1969 as a funk ensemble, exponents of gritty funk and rock, coated with sticky horns. In time, Lionel's skill at writing the perfect pop ballad commanded a transition

SAM COOKE

Sam Cooke epitomized the classic qualities of greatness and both inspired and influenced generations of soul singers. In the present climate of black music, it is hard to imagine that we will ever see the likes of him again, an artist who, through his music, was a voice for the people, a natural down-to-earth communicator.

The Commodores missed their lead singer Lionel Richie.

As in the tradition of most great soul singers, Sam came through the church and indeed most of his best work was with his gospel group the Soul Stirrers, but from his secular work songs like 'You Send Me' and 'A Change Is Gonna Come' remain soul classics. He was the definitive soul singer, tragically shot under mysterious circumstances at a motel when he was just 29 years old.

He was born in Chicago in 1931, and established his vocal credentials on the gospel scene before turning to secular music, initially under the name Dale Cooke. He officially turned solo as Sam Cooke in 1957 with the hit 'You Send Me', the first in a string of hits which established him as an international soul star.

RANDY CRAWFORD

A talented lady with a unique voice, Randy Crawford is one of the great voices in modern soul and has inspired both fans and contemporary soul singers since the Seventies. She has truly got to be one of the most inspired vocalists in the history of black music. Never blatantly directing her music to suit the day, Randy has always channelled her expression, it would seem, in an honest and personable way. She encompasses all the expressive, heartfelt qualities of a classic soul singer, but with it she possesses a spiritual, ethereal element uncommon in other black female singers. She has one of the most distinctive voices among soul artists of her time, and with time should be further recognized for these special qualities of hers.

Born in Macon, Georgia in 1952, Randy grew up in Cincinnati, Ohio, and gained early singing experience in church and at school. In 1972 she was given her first major break by George Benson who invited her to tour as his opening act and in 1976 helped secure her a record deal with Warner Brothers where she records through to this day. It was, however, her guest appearance with the Crusaders on 'Street Life' that brought attention to her on a major commercial level.

WILL DOWNING

Will Downing is one of the few major vocal talents who evolved in the late Eighties. He has already released three successful albums in the UK, and although this New Yorker has yet to match this success at home in the US, he is likely to be a major international name in soul music through the Nineties. Though initially compared with Luther Vandross, in hindsight his voice shows enough individuality and uniqueness to be recognized in his own right as a truly great balladeer. It would appear through his latter works that he is developing his musical expression more honestly and in doing so has gained great respect for his commitment to his artistry.

He originally worked as a New York session singer before street-wise dance music producer Arthur Baker hired him as lead singer for Wall Jump Jnr. Arthur later took him to Island Records and produced the first in his series of album releases.

THE DRIFTERS

The Drifters are an important group in the story of soul music in that their records took R&B's first irrevocable step towards what was to become known as soul music in the Sixties. In particular, when Leiber and Stoller produced 'There Goes My Baby' in 1959, R&B progressed from being the marriage of doo-wop with perhaps a live band, to a more producer orientated form of music with strings, horns and the utilization of new studio techniques.

The group inspired a generation of groups and singers, and were originally formed in 1953 to showcase the vocals of original lead singer Clyde McPhatter. Alongside Gerhard Thrasher, Andrew Thrasher and Bill Pinkney, the Drifters worked with Atlantic Records' Jerry Wexler and founder Ahmet Ertegun on 'Money Honey' which established the group on the burgeoning rock 'n' roll scene of the Fifties.

After the departure of Clyde in 1955, the group continued with replacement lead singers David Baughn and Johnny Moore before the Sixties heyday of the group with Ben E. King fronting a new line-up of singers.

* * *

EARTH WIND AND FIRE

While James Brown, George Clinton and Sly Stone did much to create a new kind of complex music, opening up a whole new world of studio production possibilities and coining the term "funk" for their efforts, it was Earth Wind And Fire who moulded and polished this music into something super slick, radio-friendly and appealing to international dance-floors and record buyers. Combining African folk, soul and jazz with skittering horns, bright keyboards, driving rhythms and powerful vocals on

Colourful imusic and colourful live in concert, Earth Wind And Fire sparkled in the Seventies with hits like 'Fantasy' and 'Saturday Night'.

1941), who with brother Verdine White (bass), and vocalist Philip Bailey has been the nucleus of the group through to the present day.

EN VOGUE

En Vogue are presently one of the most successful groups in soul/pop crossover music and undoubtedly possess some exceptional vocal skills. In many ways they stem from the tradition of successful girl groups like Sister Sledge, the Three Degrees and the Supremes that went before them, but they are also forerunners of black girl groups of their time in that they clearly take advantage of the many new visual mediums now available which are particularly important in the promotion and marketing of Nineties black music.

Musically they have a sound which adapts well to both the dance-floor and the airwaves, but whether their music stands the test of time remains to be seen. They are very much a band of their time.

The group are Dawn Robinson from Connecticut, Terry Ellis from Texas, Cindy Herron from San Francisco and Maxine Jones from New Jersey, who first worked together under the direction of Club Nouveau's producers Denzil Foster and Thomas McElroy in 1988. They have been scoring hits on both sides of the Atlantic since 'Hold On' in 1990.

outstanding songs, Earth Wind And Fire became one of the super groups of the Seventies and took funk to unprecedented commercial heights.

Additionally, they were more than just a group in the conventional sense, in that they developed new artists (e.g. Deniece Williams and the Emotions) of which many have become recognized in their own right, while in concert their stage shows incorporated magic, visual illusions and impressive special effects which made them one of the most colourful and exciting groups to catch live.

The group was founded in 1970 by Maurice White (drums/percussion/kalimba/vocals, born in Chicago in

ROBERTA FLACK

Possessing one of black soul music's most unusual voices, Roberta Flack is recognized and respected for her individual and personable approach as a singer. She delivers songs with a sensitive, underspoken, almost white vocal style which, married to an equally individual repertoire, makes her particularly original. Similar to Randy Crawford, she shows an integrity to her craft uncommon among her contemporaries.

She was born in Black Mountain, North Carolina, in 1939 but grew up in Arlington, Virginia, where she won a music scholarship to Howard University having taken piano lessons since the age of 9.

Her classmate was Donny Hathaway with whom she later recorded, while it was jazz pianist Les McCann who first recognized her vocal talent and enlisted her services professionally once she had moved to Washington.

Atlantic Records signed her in 1969 and released her album *First Take* from which 'The First Time Ever I Saw Your Face' eventually reached the charts in 1972 and established her as a major new soul voice.

THE FOUR TOPS

See separate entry in the Legends section.

Roberta Flack is one of the most recognized and respected vocalists in soul music, coupling outstanding music with hit records.

ARETHA FRANKLIN

See separate entry in the Legends section.

MARVIN GAYE

See separate entry in the Legends section.

GLORIA GAYNOR

Gloria Gaynor was one of the first big-voiced divas of disco, her powerful vocals having the ability to dominate even the most over-produced of the dance music show tunes which were her speciality.

She was born in Newark, New Jersey, in 1949 and turned professional as a teenager as a member of local group the Soul Satisfiers. Discovered in New York, she recorded briefly for Columbia before MGM/Polydor signed her in 1974 and launched her career with a pre-disco outing 'Honey Bee'.

As disco became flavour of the moment, Gloria's career went from strength to strength and hits flowed with 'Never Can Say Goodbye', 'Reach Out I'll Be There', 'All I Need Is Your Sweet Lovin'', 'How High The Moon', 'This Love Affair', 'I Will Survive' and 'Let Me Know I Have The Right'.With the demise of disco, Gloria maintained her following among gay audiences and in

1983 delivered the ultimate gay anthem 'I Am What I Am' from *La Cage Aux Folles* which gave her an international hit and an enthusiastic club following.

AL GREEN

Al Green is a soul singer in the true sense of the word who can so clearly communicate the most vulnerable and sensitive emotions less commonly expressed in songs by other male singers. It was his inventive, tetchy and often breathy vocal style which, with the help of his producer Willie Mitchell and exceptional musicianship, made him one of soul music's greats. By the mid-Seventies he had sold 30 million records!

He was born in Forest City, Alabama, in 1946, and in 1964 formed the Creations, later to become Al Green And The Soul Mates. While their single 'Back Up Train' sold 400,000 copies, follow-ups failed and Al's career was saved by Willie Mitchell who persuaded him to go and work for the Hi label in Memphis.

In 1969, his version of 'I Can't Get Next To You', already a hit for the Temptations, reflected Al's unique vocal style so well that it brought him instant recognition. He had also written his own first million-seller '(I'm So) Tired Of Being Alone' by 1971.

The timing of Al's success couldn't have been better for the Memphis soul scene which had started to fall apart following the demise of the Stax/Volt labels. The new energy rescued a number of musicians who contributed towards Willie Mitchell's country-edged post-Stax style which he utilized on Al's records. Drummer Al Jackson in particular should also be noted for his outstanding work in perfectly complementing Al Green's voice on his numerous soul classics such as 'Let's Stay Together' and 'I'm Still In Love With You'.

DONNY HATHAWAY

Donny Hathaway was a visionary songwriter, exceptional musician and talented vocalist. Although not one of the most highlighted names in black male singers of his time, ironically since then he has gained enormous respect for his truly exceptional individual and soulful singing. As true of many artists, Donny Hathaway's somewhat insecure and complex nature, combined with his obvious talents, was the source of his inspiration. The trouble in his life was clearly reflected through his work, and is often quoted by up-and-coming artists as being a major influence on their own creativity.

He was born in Chicago in 1945 and, with university room mate Leroy Hutson, co-wrote the jazz fusion classic 'The Ghetto', while achieving his greatest commercial success alongside Roberta Flack on duets 'Where Is The Love' (1972), 'The Closer I Get To You' (1978) and 'Back Together Again' (1980). His best remembered solo work is perhaps 'Someday We'll All Be Free', a soul classic recorded by numerous artists over the years, and the exceptional *Extensions Of A Man* album.

ISAAC HAYES

To most people, the name Isaac Hayes will conjure up memories of both the sound-track music he composed to the film *Shaft* (the most successful blaxploitation movie), and the lead role he played in the film and its sequels during the Seventies. His career, however, goes back to the Sixties when he worked as a session musician with Otis Redding and composed a number of the Stax label's biggest sellers.

He was born in Covington, Tennessee, in 1938. After developing his skills as a multi-instrumentalist he was hired in the mid-Sixties by the Stax label where in collaboration with David Porter he wrote the classic 'Soul Man' for Sam And Dave alongside a string of R&B hits and classics for Carla Thomas, Mable John, Wilson Pickett, Don Covay, the Soul Children and the Emotions.

As a recording artist he first recorded a solo album in 1967, *Presenting Isaac Hayes*, but first charted with *Hot Buttered Soul* (the name he subsequently used for his group of backing vocalists). The album featured a version of the Glen Campbell hit 'By The Time I Get To Phoenix', an American hit single which truly showcased the deep throated crooning voice which became one of his trademarks. Overall, the track also laid foundations of a style Barry White was later to have such success with.

HEATWAVE

Heatwave is a multinational, interracial group that was formed by Dayton, Ohio-born brothers Johnnie and Keith Wilder in Germany during the mid-Seventies. Their success can be clearly attributed to the exceptional songwriting of Rod Temperton, the group's original keyboard player who, from 1976, turned in hits 'Boogie Nights', 'The Groove Line' and 'Always And Forever' before leaving to write more hits for Michael Jackson, Donna Summer, Quincy Jones, Rufas, Mica Paris and numerous others.

Tragedy struck in 1979 when Johnnie became paraplegic after a car accident, but the group continued to record albums successfully through to 1982. They regrouped in 1990 on the Brothers Organization label for a remake of 'Mind Blowing Decisions'.

Members in the group over the years have included Tommy Harris (drums), Ernest "Bilbo" Berger (drums), Eric Johns (guitar), Billy Jones (guitar), Mario Mantese (bass), Derek Bramble (bass), Roy Carter (bass), and J. D. Nicholas (vocals).

✷　✷　✷

With the looks, the voice and the star appeal, Whitney reflects the commercial face of soul music in the Eighties and Nineties.

WHITNEY HOUSTON

Truly the black female superstar of the Eighties, Whitney Houston is as perfect a representation of the ideal of young black America, combining talent, beauty, youth, and success, as Diana Ross was to her generation. While possessing an excellent voice, especially for the pop idiom, Whitney is unlikely to be remembered or heralded as one of the great female voices in soul music. She is, however, a soul star.

She was born in 1963, the daughter of Cissy Houston and niece of Dionne Warwick, and took her early vocal coaching at the New Hope Baptist Church where her mother was minister of music.

She began her professional career as a model, lending her slender figure and good looks to the pages of *Cosmopolitan* and *Seventeen* while simultaneously taking her gospel-trained vocals into clubland where she came to the attention of Arista Records' president Clive Davis. Signed to Arista in 1983, her début album *Whitney Houston* sold over 13 million copies worldwide and established her as an international star.

PHYLLIS HYMAN

Phyllis Hyman came to the fore as an artist in the late Seventies, when songs 'Living Inside Your Love', 'Under Your Spell' and particularly 'You Know How To Love Me' introduced her to both dance-floor audiences and soul fans. One of the most sophisticated, subtle and stylish soul/jazz singers, Phyllis, although not having major chart success, has gained an enormous and growing loyal following for her quality as a singer and for her work.

She was born in Pittsburgh, raised in Philadelphia, and began her professional career in 1971 with a group called the New Direction. Moving to New York she won over club audiences and in 1976 was hired by jazz-funk instrumentalist/producer Norman Connors to be a featured vocalist on his album *You Are My Starship* for Buddah Records. She continues to record with Norman.

Her solo career took off in 1977, initially signed to Buddah and then Arista where in 1979 she teamed up with one of the hottest dance/R&B production teams of the day—Mtume and Lucas—at the most prolific point of her career with both soul and dance audiences. She currently records for Philadelphia International Records.

THE IMPRESSIONS

Vocal group the Impressions were formed in Chicago by Curtis Mayfield and Jerry Butler. Sam Gooden with brothers Richard and Arthur Brooks completed the line-up, and from 1958 the group took their initial musical influence from the secular R&B direction from which the Drifters were coming, while vocally it launched a solo career for its lead singer Jerry Butler. Fred Cash replaced Jerry, though it was Curtis Mayfield who became the group's lead singer, establishing his own unique high tenor vocal style on their 1961 hit single for Paramount Records 'Gypsy Woman'.

The group were reduced to a trio in 1962 on the departure of the Brooks brothers, but continued to score numerous American hits including 'People Get Ready' (1965), the song which expressed the concerns Curtis felt for the civil rights movement and the black church, and established him as a social commentator.

Curtis Mayfield left the Impressions in 1970, by which time he had formed his own Curtom label, and appointed Leroy Hutson as the group's new lead singer.

JAMES INGRAM

James Ingram's unique vocal style was first noticed by Quincy Jones who appointed him as a featured vocalist on his platinum album *The Dude* (1981) on hit songs 'Just Once' and 'One Hundred Ways'.

James was born in Ohio and had originally moved to Los Angeles in 1973 to be a session musician. Before his break with Quincy he had been a keyboard player for Leon Haywood and his own group Revelation Funk. After *The Dude*, Quincy signed him to his Qwest label and in 1983 released what was to be his solo chart début 'Yah Mo B There'. James also worked with Patti Austin in 1983 to produce the hit duet 'Baby Come To Me'.

James's solo work continued with the album *Never Felt So Good* (1986), produced by Keith Diamond, following

which he signed directly to Warner Brothers for a 1989 album *It's Real*, the title track being the epitome of swing beat (produced by Gene Griffin).

Elsewhere James wrote 'P.Y.T. (Pretty Young Thing)' for Michael Jackson and was a featured singer on the Quincy Jones hit 'The Secret Garden' from the album *Back On The Block* (1989).

After being the voice of Mystic Merlin, Freddie Jackson delivered the ultimate pop soul ballad in 'Rock Me Tonight', but has yet to repeat such success.

ISLEY BROTHERS

See separate entry in the Legends section.

FREDDIE JACKSON

Freddie Jackson became one of the Eighties' premier male soul vocalists in 1985, delivering the hit ballad 'Rock Me Tonight' from the first of a string of platinum albums. Although this first entry into the public eye showed great potential, since then he has never managed to build on his initial promise and has been overshadowed by newer artists.

He was born in Harlem, New York, and sang at the White Rock Baptist Church before entering the music business as a session singer in the mid-Seventies. His first major recording break came in 1982 when the group Mystic Merlin appointed him lead singer for their *Full Moon* album for Capitol Records which featured the popular soul tune 'Mr. Magician'.

Capitol signed him as a solo artist in 1985 from which time he has maintained popularity as balladeer on the adult R&B scene with songs including 'You Are My Lady' (his UK chart début in 1985), 'Tasty Love' (1986), 'Have You Ever Loved Somebody' (1986), 'Nice 'N' Slow' (1988), 'Crazy (For Me)' (1988), 'Don't It Feel Good' (1990) and 'Me And Mrs Jones' (1992). In 1993 he changed labels to RCA.

JANET JACKSON

As younger sister to Michael Jackson, Janet carved a career in acting and toyed with music before the failure of a brief marriage to James Debarge sent her to Minneapolis to take the music business by storm. She became the first artist to claim a song-writing share with writers/producers Jimmy Jam and Terry Lewis who collaborated on *Control*, her first multi-platinum album. She is more recognized for her role as a performer than for her ability as a singer, although she has a distinctive vocal style that's well suited to the placement of her music.

She is the youngest of nine Jackson children and was born in Gary, Indiana, in 1966. In 1973 she made her stage début alongside her brothers in Las Vegas, then aged 10 played the role of Penny Gordon Woods in the American TV series *Good Times*.

After a spell in the cast of *Different Strokes* (1980–2) she signed to A&M where she has since became one of the Eighties' most successful black artists. The Nineties await her new affiliation with Virgin Records.

One of the most successful recording artists of the Eighties and Nineties, Janet Jackson is in control.

JERMAINE JACKSON

Jermaine Jackson is the fourth oldest of the Jackson family and both sang and played bass with the Jackson Five before embarking on a solo career.

He was born in Gary, Indiana, in 1954, joined his family's group in 1969 and married Motown president Berry Gordy's daughter Hazel in 1973. When the Jackson Five became the Jacksons in 1975 and moved labels to Epic, Jermaine stayed at Motown to pursue a solo career. After albums *My Name Is Jermaine* (1976), *Feel The Fire* (1977) and *Frontiers* (1978), Jermaine hooked up with Stevie Wonder who wrote him his biggest hit single 'Let's Get Serious' in 1980.

Further albums continued with *Jermaine* (1981), *I Like Your Style* (1981) and *Let Me Tickle Your Fancy* (1982) before he joined the Jacksons for reunion albums *Victory* (1984) and *2300 Jackson Street* (1989). He has recorded for Arista since 1984, including a duet with Whitney Houston 'Take Good Care Of My Heart' on her début album.

MICHAEL JACKSON

Michael Jackson is one of the most successful artists in the history of recorded music and with *Thriller* achieved the biggest-selling album of all time. In the Nineties he is generally regarded as a "pop" star and not acclaimed quite so much as a soul vocalist, but one can't ignore his

roots and the fact that he was an accomplished balladeer by the age of 12 when his voice had more
soul than many on the soul scene today.

As a singer today he is overshadowed by his
larger-than-life performance videos and stage
shows, thus becoming less recognized
for what were once inspirational,
untampered-with natural and innocent vocals. But it must be said that
artistically he is a genius.

He was born in Gary,
Indiana, in 1958, the sev-
enth of nine children,
and joined his brothers in
the Jackson Five at the
age of 10. In 1970 the
maturity of his vocals
was already staggering
and through the early
Seventies he gave per-
formances which
many would consider
to be far more soulful
than anything you are
likely to hear today.

The most successful artist in the history of recorded music, Michael Jackson
is a genius of popular music.

58

THE JACKSON FIVE (THE JACKSONS)

The Jacksons have become one of the most successful show-business families of all time, with Michael, Janet and Jermaine three major recording artists in their own right. All are children of Joe Jackson who formed the group in 1966. Michael, Jermaine, Marlon, Jackie and Tito from Gary, Indiana, first recorded locally as the Little Jackson Brothers before Bobby Taylor saw them perform and brought them to the attention of Motown Records in 1968. Naming them the Jackson Five, Bobby wrote and produced their hits 'I Want You Back', 'ABC', and 'The Love You Save', establishing the brothers internationally and introducing a new dimension to Motown.

For a decade the group rode smoothly through the transition of the Motown sound of the Sixties to the Philly sound of the Seventies due primarily to some fine song-writing and the incredible vocal skills of lead singer Michael. When Michael's voice broke, the group still remained on top of things through the late Seventies disco era with songs 'Blame It On The Boogie' and 'Shake Your Body (Down To The Ground)', before the spotlight was turned on his solo career.

RICK JAMES

Rick James was successful from the late Seventies through to the mid Eighties with his own unique sound which fused funk and soul with lashings of horns and synthesizers. Similar to many full-bodied dance-floor production styles of that time (Earth Wind And Fire, Mtume and Lucas, Gamble and Huff, etc.), this sound didn't make a comfortable transition to where technology took dance music from the late Eighties, but Rick in his heyday had a formula which he successfully applied not only to his own music, but to his various spin-offs too, including the Mary Jane Girls ('All Night Long'), Teena Marie ('I'm A Sucker For Your Love'), Val Young, the Temptations and the Stone City Band.

Born James Johnson in Buffalo, New York, in 1955, in the late Sixties he formed a group, the Mynah Birds, with the then unknown Neil Young in Canada. Moving briefly to London he formed a blues band, Main Line, before heading for Los Angeles where he signed to Berry Gordy's Motown label in 1978.

His most successful singles commercially were 'You And I' and 'Give It To Me Baby', but his other memorable moments include 'Dance Wit' Me', 'Standing On The Top', 'Ebony Eyes' (a duet with Smokey Robinson), 'Glow' and 'The Flag'.

AL JARREAU

A jazz singer who over the years has broadened his appeal to soul audiences, Al Jarreau has also enjoyed commercial pop success.

Al Jarreau is an artist who appeals to both soul and jazz audiences and uses his voice as a musical instrument in what is called "scatting", in addition to singing in the traditional sense.

He was born in Milwaukee, Wisconsin, in 1940, and studied psychology at university before becoming the resident singer at the Half-Note Club in San Francisco, along with pianist George Duke, in the mid-Sixties. He was signed by the Reprise Records/Warner Brothers in 1975 and embarked on a series of albums which initially sold most to jazz audiences, but from his *This Time* album (1980) he appealed more to soul/R&B fans with songs including 'Spain' and 'Distracted'.

His most acclaimed soul album is *Breakin' Away* (including 'Easy', 'Roof Garden' and 'We're In This Love Together'), although commercially the pop appeal of his *Jarreau* album granted him hits with 'Mornin'', 'Trouble In Paradise' and 'Boogie Down'. His next best album was the Nile Rodgers-produced *L Is For Love* (1986), although his next chart hit was 'Moonlighting' (1987), the theme to the eponymous TV series, which remains by far his most successful release.

GLENN JONES

Glenn Jones is one of the finest contemporary purveyors of adult R&B/soul music, but has to date not found the record to grant him the commercial success Luther Vandross, Freddie Jackson and Alexander O'Neal have found in this field. Instead he has a loyal following, especially on the UK soul scene, who have supported his consistently high quality recordings since he first sang 'Melancholy Fire' for Norman Connors in 1980.

He was born in Jacksonville, Florida, and grew up in an environment of gospel music. He formed his own gospel group the Modulations when he was just 14 and even made two albums with the group—*James Cleveland Presents The Modulations* (1975) and *Feel The Fire* (1976)—for the Savoy label.

Drummer/jazz-funk producer Norman Connors gave Glenn a break in the secular music field in 1980 by featuring him as a vocalist on his album *Take It To The Limit*, and by 1983 he was signed to the RCA label where his début solo release was the impressive mini-album *Everybody Loves A Winner*.

EDDIE KENDRICKS

Eddie Kendricks possessed one of the most unusual male singing voices; the soft, gentle, almost feminine qualities of his voice made his silky vocal style one of the most recognized of his time. His success came predominantly as a member of the Temptations and his lead performance on the Motown classic 'Just My Imagination' is his best-remembered work.

He was born in Birmingham, Alabama, in 1940, but was drawn to Detroit

The voice of the Temptations on 'Just My Imagination'.

in the late Fifties by the thriving music scene soon shown to the world by Motown Records. Eddie worked with a number of vocal groups in the city before he made his mark with the Temptations on hits including 'The Way You Do The Things You Do' and 'Just My Imagination' during his brief spell with the group in 1970–1.

As a solo artist, 'Keep On Truckin'' (1973) was both his most successful and most memorable hit, although songs including 'Date With The Rain', 'Boogie Down', 'Shoeshine Boy', 'Happy', and 'He's A Friend' obtained a degree of success on the Tamla/Motown label.

CHAKA KHAN

Chaka Khan has to be the most innovative and respected songstress in modern black music, her vocal style and capabilities setting a standard that has yet to be matched, although sought by many. Her music crosses and links many styles, while her vocal expression is able to convey from the purest to the wildest of emotions. She is truly a genius and second to none.

Chaka (real name Yvette Marie Stevens) is also one of the few great singers not to have come through the church, the night club scene in her hometown Chicago (where she was born in 1953) giving her the experience and the appetite for a professional career in music which began for her in the late Sixties.

In 1971 she became lead singer of America's premier funk/rock group Rufus and first came to prominence in

61

Chaka Khan, vocally one of the most accomplished of all soul singers, was the voice of Rufus, one of the most innovative groups of the Seventies.

the United States when Stevie Wonder penned their first hit 'Tell Me Something Good', although it was her Ashford and Simpson-produced début solo hit 'I'm Every Woman' which established her internationally in 1978.

BEN E. KING

Ben E. King plays an important role in the history of soul as a songwriter, lead singer of the Drifters (from 1959), and solo artist.

He was born Benjamin Earl Nelson in Henderson, North Carolina, in 1938, but moved to New York in 1947. At high school he sang with the Moonglows before joining vocal group the Five Crowns, who were recruited as a complete new line-up of the Drifters in 1959.

While with the Drifters, the most successful R&B group of the late Fifties, Ben wrote 'There Goes My Baby' which virtually changed the face of soul music with its innovative use of strings by producers Jerry Leiber and Mike Stoller. Ben was also lead singer on the record, leading them again on the 1960 hit 'Save The Last Dance For Me'.

As a solo artist he is important for 'Spanish Harlem' (1960) and 'Stand By Me' (1961), which again epitomize the work of producers Leiber and Stoller (predecessors to Holland, Dozier and Holland, Gamble and Huff, Jam and Lewis and other great partnerships over the years),

and are simply great soul classics (especially 'Stand By Me' which he co-wrote and was a UK Number 1 hit again in 1987).

EVELYN "CHAMPAGNE" KING

The initial promise of Evelyn's début 'Shame' brought with it great excitement on the music scene. Her mature and commanding performance did not reflect her young years, and the production transcended the disco music of its time to become a timeless dance-floor classic. Vocally, however, Evelyn's development through the years has not been as great as perhaps was expected, although she has consistently made successful albums in between the occasional hit.

She was born in the Bronx, New York, in 1960, her father being a member of two vocal groups. In 1970 the family moved to Philadelphia where she was discovered while working as a cleaning lady at Sigma Sound Studios.

Her début single 'Shame' was a multi-million worldwide seller and one of the very first 12-inch singles when it was released in the UK in 1978. It was produced by Philadelphia artist/producer T-Life and was her only hit until 1982 when she teamed up with the hottest R&B team of the day, Mighty M Productions, who gave Evelyn her biggest hit single, and another dance classic 'Love Come Down'.

GLADYS KNIGHT AND THE PIPS

Gladys Knight has to represent undoubtedly the closest approximation of a true soul singer. Encompassing such qualities as warmth, compassion and honesty, she communicates life's experiences with an intimacy and an empathy matched by no other. Over the 40 years that she has offered her heart and soul, she deserves her place as one of the greatest exponents of her art.

She was born in Atlanta, Georgia, in 1944 and won a major singing contest at the age of 7 before forming Gladys Knight And The Pips with brother Merald and cousins William Guest and Edward Patten at the ripe old age of 9. Just 3 years later they were touring professionally with Sam Cooke and Jackie Wilson and recording songs for a number of local labels.

In 1966 they signed to the Soul label (a Motown subsidiary) in Detroit and made the charts with songs including 'I Heard It Through The Grapevine' (later a hit again for Marvin Gaye) before Gladys became the true artist we know today, emoting boldly on her first adult love ballad 'If I Were Your Woman' (1970). The song was the first to break her from the confines of the formularized "Motown sound" of the Sixties and for the early Seventies established Gladys as the black Barbra Streisand. She remains a genuine soul star in the Nineties.

KOOL AND THE GANG

Kool And The Gang was one of the first fully-fledged funk ensembles to emerge in the early Seventies, but after a major transition in the late Seventies became one of the most successful pop/soul groups of the Eighties.

Brothers Robert "Kool" Bell (bass) and Ronald Bell (sax/keyboards) from New Jersey first formed a group the Jazziacs with a couple of friends in 1964 and worked as session musicians in New York before forming Kool And The Gang in 1969.

With the addition of Charles Smith (guitar), Dennis "Dee Tee" Thomas (alto sax), Robert "Spike" Mickens (trumpet), Clifford Adams (trombone) and Michael Ray (trumpet), the group became purveyors of earthy funk, and innovators in their use of slick horns and vocal chants.

The group's move to mainstream pop couldn't have been more dramatic. With the addition of a lead vocalist in 1979, they employed the services of Brazilian producer Eumir Deodato who moulded them a much less spontaneously live, more refined studio sound.

The resulting *Ladies' Night* album launched the group on the path to international stardom and success with hits which, with time, owed less to the group's black R&B roots and more to the white pop idiom. It later launched a solo career for lead singer J. T. Taylor.

PATTI LABELLE

One of the most unusual voices in the business, Patti appealed more to soul audiences as a solo artist after working in a group with a predominantly rock appeal.

One of the most distinctive and respected vocalists, Patti Labelle possesses a voice unlike any other. With her great range, control and flexibility, Patti may not have one of the most natural-sounding voices in soul terms, but definitely one of the most original. She comes to her best in her live performances, always managing to surprise her audiences with not just her greatness as a singer but with her larger-than-life character and image.

She was born Patricia Holt in Philadelphia in 1944, and scored a million-selling hit in America with 'I Sold My Heart To The Junkman' (1961) as lead singer with the Blue Belles. Through the mid-Sixties she carved a following among R&B but predominantly rock audiences with hit songs including 'Cold Water', 'Decateur Street' and 'Down The Aisle'. When the group became simply Labelle they scored their biggest hit 'Lady Marmalade (Voulez-Vous Coucher Avec Moi Ce Soir)' (1975), perhaps Patti's best-remembered performance.

Patti went solo in 1977, since when she has appealed less to rock audiences and steadily more to R&B audiences, epitomized by her duets with Bobby Womack and her albums for the Philadelphia International label with producers Kenny Gamble, Leon Huff and Dexter Wansel. Her biggest recent hit was 'On My Own'.

LEVERT

While the O'Jays are currently an American institution, Levert are one of the most successful pioneers of contemporary Nineties soul and could well be held in equally high esteem by future generations. The connection? Brothers Gerald and Sean Levert are the sons of the lead singer of the O'Jays, Eddie Levert. Together with Marc Gordon, Levert took shape in the mid-Eighties and were early instigators of the new jack swing sound which has come into its own and dominated the R&B scene in the Nineties. That is not, however, how the band started out.

Originally from Ohio, Gerald, Sean and Marc made their recording début in 1985 for the Tempre label in Philadelphia when their style was much of a cross between Maze and the O'Jays themselves.

Signing to Atlantic Records in 1986, their *Bloodline* album delivered a US Number 1 R&B single with '(Pop Pop Pop Pop) Goes My Mind' before they scored success in the UK with 'Casanova' in 1987. From here the group experimented with new jack swing, moving into production themselves for a number of other R&B artists on the scene (including James Ingram, Miki Howard, Rude Boys and Stephanie Mills).

Meanwhile lead singer Gerald Levert (who sounds particularly like his father) launched a solo career in 1991 with an album *Private Line*.

JOHNNY MATHIS

Much like Nat King Cole, Johnny Mathis comes from a more classic era of the song form, and not so much from the tradition of soul music. However, being so highly respected for his voice and masterly conveyance of song, he has managed to bring much of his music to soul audiences, more noticeably on duets with artists such as Deniece Williams, Dionne Warwick and Gladys Knight. It would be fair, though, to say that he seems more suited and satisfied in his initial musical direction.

He was born in San Francisco in 1935 and has been notching up pop hits since the late Fifties, although he is perhaps best remembered for his interpretation of 'Misty', his first Sixties hit. Although incredibly successful thereafter, it was not until 1978 that he was recognized in R&B circles for his work with Deniece Williams on duets 'Too Much Too Little Too Late'

Johnny Mathis was a classic rather than typical soul singer.

and 'You're All I Need To Get By'. In 1979 he toyed with disco on what became a hit 'Gone Gone Gone', before a soul duet with Gladys Knight gave him another hit record in 1981 with 'When A Child Is Born'.

CURTIS MAYFIELD

Curtis Mayfield is truly a veteran and classic soul artist whose career spans close on 40 years, during which time he has enjoyed success as both lead singer with the Impressions and as a solo artist.

He was born in Chicago in 1942 and formed the Impressions in the late Fifties, fronting the group with his distinctive near-falsetto voice for a string of US hits before launching his own Curtom Records company in 1968 in order to cultivate local talent and give himself a better vehicle to express his strong views on the black issues of the day.

In 1970 he embarked on a solo career where he further pursued the socially conscious depictions of urban black street life. His songs became sermonettes on drugs, war, racism, the environment and religion. While Marvin Gaye is often credited for inspiring the whole range of socially-conscious soul singers in the Seventies, Curtis was preaching about the concerns of the civil rights movement and other political issues on songs like 'A Change Is Gonna Come' and the aforementioned 'People Get Ready' with the Impressions back in the mid-Sixties.

MAZE, FEATURING FRANKIE BEVERLY

Maze have consistently made soul albums since the early Seventies, pampering little to the music of the day and essentially making good, down-home honest soul music for their international audience of soul fans. They are best remembered for a live recording of their 1980 soul anthem 'Joy And Pain'.

The group, comprising a nucleus of Wayne Thomas (guitar), Sam Porter (keyboards), Robin Duhe (bass), Roame Lowry (congas/vocals) and McKinley "Bug" Williams (percussion/vocals), is essentially a vehicle for their founder, chief member and lead vocalist Frankie Beverly to exploit the songwriting skills he first explored with earlier groups the Butlers and Raw Soul during the Sixties and early Seventies.

Maze was originally formed in Philadelphia during 1971, but Frankie relocated the group to San Francisco shortly thereafter so as not to get caught up in the burgeoning "Philly sound" under the control of producers Gamble and Huff. Signing to Capitol in 1976 they released a series of albums from which 'Golden Time Of Day' (1978), 'Feel That You're Feelin'' (1979), 'Southern Girl' and 'The Look In Your Eyes' (1980), were among the songs which built their profile before the aforementioned 'Joy And Pain' brought them to the attention of a mainstream audience. They currently record for WEA.

HAROLD MELVIN AND THE BLUE NOTES

The point about Harold Melvin And The Blue Notes is that during their heyday it was Teddy Pendergrass and not Harold Melvin who was the vocalist on all the glorious Seventies Philly classics. Indeed they were unique in that the focal part in the group's name was not the focal part in the group itself. Thus, when Teddy left to form a solo career, Harold and his replacement struggled to maintain the level of success.

The group had evolved from the street corners of Philadelphia during the mid-Fifties, but the turning-point came when Philly moguls Gamble and Huff finally signed a lucrative label deal with the mighty CBS Records and were able to invest fully in the immense local talent

The lead voice of Harold Melvin And The Blue Notes was rarely Harold Melvin, the group grooming Teddy Pendergrass for solo stardom in the late Seventies.

around them. Harold Melvin And The Blue Notes (Teddy Pendergrass, Dwight Johnson, Jerry Cummings and William Spratley) were signed to the Philadelphia International label in 1972 and scored international success on classics including 'If You Don't Know Me By Now', 'The Love I Lost', 'Wake Up Everybody', and 'Don't Leave Me This Way', all of which typified Gamble and Huff's supreme command of words to convey timeless situations with infectious melodies and full-bodied productions. They are currently on the comeback track having re-signed to Philadelphia International.

MIDNIGHT STAR

A self-contained soul/funk group, Midnight Star are interesting in that they came to prominence during the dying days of disco and lasted the transition through experimental electro-funk of the early Eighties and beyond to the instigation of the earliest forms of new jack swing now prominent in the Nineties.

They were formed in 1976 at Kentucky State University by brothers Reggie Calloway (trumpet/flute/percussion) and Vincent Calloway (trombone/trumpet/percussion) who were the driving force behind the group's success. The group also consisted of fellow students Belinda Lipscomb (lead vocals), Melvin Watson (lead vocals), Boaz "Bo" Watson (lead vocals/keyboards), Jeffrey Cooper (lead guitar/keyboards), Kenneth Gant (bass/vocals), Bobby Lovelace (drums) and William Simmons (sax/keyboards/percussion).

Based in Los Angeles during the Eighties, they are best remembered in soul circles for their song 'Curious' and on a pop level for 'Headlines' and 'Midas Touch' before the Calloway brothers left the group and became successful producers for Levert ('Casanova'), Natalie Cole ('Jump Start'), and Gladys Knight And The Pips ('Love Overboard') among others.

STEPHANIE MILLS

"Exciting", "thrilling" and "captivating" are terms that depict some of the most distinctive qualities of this unique singer. She expresses herself with a passion and determination to reach the hearts and souls of her listeners, her musical forms ranging from show songs through to classic soul and dance music. She was born in New York in 1957 and landed a professional role on Broadway at the age of 9 in *Maggie Flynn*. Her most famous stage role, however, is as Dorothy in *The Wiz*, which she first took at the age of 17 and performed for 4 years before recent reunion dates.

As a recording artist her biggest commercial hit is 'Never Knew Love Like This Before', a song produced by Mtume and Lucas in their Seventies heyday. On a pop level she is also remembered for the mid-Eighties 'The Medicine Song'.

Stephanie also presented a daily show on NBC, returned frequently to the role of Dorothy in *The Wiz* and is one of the few lucky performers who has recorded consistently through to this day.

One of soul music's more unusual voices, Stephanie Mills made it through the Broadway stage rather than the traditional church route.

BILLY OCEAN

Billy Ocean is unusual in that he became a major black star without having one of the most outstanding voices, and in the UK, a place not known for breaking soul artists. Highly successful in the US and UK, he has made his mark, albeit in a pop/soul vein with the help of catchy songs that have appealed to the general public in a big way. He proves that it takes more than a great voice to be successful and that well-chosen material, a striking personality and image, together with the support of major record label investment, count for a great deal more.

His real name is Les Charles and he was born in Trinidad in 1950, before moving with his family to London in 1968. His recording career took off in 1976 with the release of the hit 'Love Really Hurts Without You', but greater success came from 1984 when a change of label to Jive and the release of 'Caribbean Queen' propelled him to superstardom with soul, but mainly pop, audiences on both sides of the Atlantic.

THE O'JAYS

The O'Jays are an American institution and have been at the heart of US black music for 30 years. Originally Eddie Levert, Walter Williams, Bobby Massey and William Powell, they scored their first hit, 'Lonely Drifter', with Bill Isles (from Canton, Ohio) in 1963,

and through the Seventies were at the forefront of Philadelphia's soul movement through an extremely successful liaison with writers/producers Kenny Gamble and Leon Huff on songs like 'Love Train', 'I Love Music' and 'Back Stabbers'. The fellow high school students first sang together as the Mascots, but after changing their name to the O'Jays, they notched up ten R&B hits for Imperial before joining forces with Gamble and Huff in 1970.

With the departure of Bobby Massey in 1971, the group signed to the Philadelphia International label where Gamble and Huff put the O'Jays in the vanguard of their hit-making machine with a new production style which changed the face of black music.

Eddie Levert's sons are Gerald and Sean Levert, two-thirds of the group Levert who have been pioneers of the new jack swing music scene. Gerald also has a solo recording career with Atlantic Records.

OMAR

Omar is new to the soul scene, but after only two years he has been cited as the Nineties' Stevie Wonder with some innovative and superbly made music produced for both himself as a singer and for other British artists.

He was born in Canterbury, Kent, in 1969, and first worked as drummer with the Kent Youth Percussion

Billy Ocean was born in Trinidad and settled in London, UK, but scored his greatest success in the US.

Ensemble/Orchestra, before joining forces with the UK independent soul label Kongo Records in 1990. His début release 'There's Nothing Like This', already regarded as a soul classic, led to a lucrative deal with Polygram's trendy Talkin' Loud label, where it became the title track of his début album in 1991.

ALEXANDER O'NEAL

Alexander O'Neal was one of the major new soul vocalists of the Eighties, his voice being a perfect vehicle to showcase the songs of writers/producers Jimmy Jam and Terry Lewis who combined mature adult songwriting with slick dance-floor grooves.

He was born in Natchez, Mississippi, in 1953, and grew up in Minneapolis where work with a number of other local groups led to a position with Flyte Time which featured Jimmy "Jam" Lewis on keyboards and Terry Lewis on guitar and bass. From 1981 the group toured extensively with Prince, but by 1985 Jam and Lewis were established in their own right and took Alex to Tabu Records to work on the albums *Alexander O'Neal, Hearsay, All True Man* and a string of hit singles.

He is another artist in a long history of soul singers who find more interest and success in the UK than in their own country (although one of the few in the late Eighties and early Nineties). But these are still early days in the career of this distinctive vocalist, who also works regularly with singer Cherrelle Week.

JEFFREY OSBORNE

Jeffrey Osborne was lead singer with the soul/funk group L.T.D. from Greensboro, North Carolina, who recorded consistently for A&M through the Seventies, including three silver albums *Something To Love* (1977), *Togetherness* (1978) and *Devotion* (1979), although they went generally unnoticed in the UK.

Jeffrey, who was born in Providence, Rhode Island, in 1951, first joined the group in 1968 as their drummer but was made lead singer in 1970. While with the group he recorded the original version of 'Love Ballad' (later a hit for George Benson), and just made the charts in 1978 with 'Holding On'.

He left the group in 1980, and signed direct to A&M in 1982 where he made an immediate impression on the soul world with songs 'On The Wings Of Love', 'I Really Don't Need No Light', and 'Don't You Get So Mad' from his first two George Duke-produced albums *Jeffrey Osborne* (1982) and *Stay With Me Tonight* (1983).

His next albums have not quite matched the promise of the first two, but were *Don't Stop* (1984), *Emotional* (1986), *One Love—One Dream* (1988), and his one album to date for Arista Records, *Only Human* (1990).

Alexander O'Neal represents the more soulful side of Minneapolis's Prince-dominated purple funk sound of the Eighties.

MICA PARIS

Mica (pronounced Meesha) Paris is without doubt the most distinctive black female singer to emerge from the UK to date. Her music presents a fine balance of maturity and street cred, her stylish and youthful image reflecting this too. She has sung classic duets with premier vocalists Bobby Womack and Will Downing, worked with Chaka Khan, and has had trendy songs written for her by Prince and Omar.

Born in south London in 1970, Mica's vocal experience came straight from the church and subsequent work as lead singer with the Spirit Of Watts gospel quintet. Her move to secular music came through liaisons with both Hollywood Beyond and the Style Council's bass player Paul Powell before 4th & Broadway/Island Records signed her as a solo artist in 1987.

Her début album *So Good* (1988) held the promise of an exciting career for Mica and included three UK hits 'My One Temptation', 'Like Dreamers Do', and 'Breathe Life Into Me'. It was a classic album, but the follow-up album *Contribution* (1989) appeared to be misdirected and it was B-side tracks 'I Should've Known Better' and 'Where Are The Children', not on the album, which attracted the most attention from the soul fraternity. We await the future with bated breath!

✳   ✳   ✳

RAY PARKER JR.

Ray Parker Jr. is best remembered for his Raydio hit 'Jack And Jill' and his biggest commercial pop hit 'Ghostbusters' (from the movie), but his colourful career in music has included being guitarist with Stevie Wonder and the Rolling Stones, while his songs have been recorded by Diana Ross, Bobby Womack and Herbie Hancock. He produced

Multi-talented, Ray Parker Jr. was a reluctant vocalist at the start of his solo career.

records for New Edition, Deniece Williams and Cheryl Lynn while also making solo recordings, including such soul gems as 'I Don't Think That Man Should Sleep Alone' and 'I Love Your Daughter' for Geffen Records.

He was born in Detroit in 1954, and first picked up a guitar after a leg injury which confined him to home. After forming a group and proving his proficiency in a city where Motown were taking the world by storm, he was hired by the Temptations, Gladys Knight And The Pips and numerous artists to work at their respective live shows. This proved an invaluable training ground.

While touring with Stevie Wonder he met the Rolling Stones who employed him between 1975 and 1977 (recording on their *Black And Blue* album). He relocated to Los Angeles and worked with Barry White prior to launching a group, Raydio, and ultimately a solo career.

DAVID PEASTON

David Peaston possesses one of the most dynamic and exceptional vocal instruments in today's black music. He has managed to place his incredible range, pitch and tone abilities best, if in a somewhat showy context, by fusing a balance of soul and jazz. An individual singer, he appeals not so much to soul music's younger audiences, but more to adult soul connoisseurs.

He was born in St Louis, the son of Martha Bass from the Clara Ward singers. He began his music career after moving to New York in 1981 and working as a session singer. His break came after a successful audition to appear at the Harlem Apollo's infamous televised talent contest introduced him to American soul audiences in 1988. The following year he was signed by Geffen Records where he worked with Anita Baker's producer Michael Powell on his début album.

Upon moving to MCA Records in 1991 he tried to appeal to younger audiences by recording a swing beat single 'String', but essentially his *Mixed Emotions* album continued his legacy of classy adult soul.

TEDDY PENDERGRASS

One of soul music's most distinctive vocals, Teddy Pendergrass exudes immense passion with a penetrating voice that stirs with a vibrant sexuality and sensuality and which makes him one of soul music's all-time great singers. Unfortunately these elements diminished somewhat after his car crash in 1982, which left him paralysed from the waist down, although he has been sounding better again with each new album.

He was born in Philadelphia in 1950 and grew up in a strictly religious environment. After being ordained as a priest in his teens and acquiring invaluable singing experience in church, he joined local group the Cadillacs as their drummer, although not for long. He was soon poached by Harold Melvin who was looking for a lead singer to front his group Harold Melvin And The Blue Notes in the late Sixties.

In 1972 the group signed to Philadelphia International, and Teddy became its lead voice during the heyday of Philly classics on songs like 'Wake Up Everybody' before he inevitably left the Blue Notes to pursue a successful solo career.

The voice of 'In The Midnight Hour', Wilson Pickett reflects the sound of mainstream soul in the Sixties.

WILSON PICKETT

Wilson Pickett wasn't the most subtle of soul singers; he sang with a growl and aggression, always with great power and with the support of great musicians from the Memphis (Stax), Detroit and Muscle Shoals stables. With his producer Jerry Wexler and the infrastructure of the mighty Atlantic Records corporation,

he was also able to cross what would otherwise be R&B hits into pop success in both the USA and UK. However his style was very much that of the Sixties era and didn't survive the transition to the funk and disco movement of the Seventies.

He was born in Prattville, Alabama, in 1942, but grew up in Detroit where he sang gospel in church before joining the Falcons with Eddie Floyd and Joe Stubbs (brother of the Four Tops' Levi Stubbs). His first solo success came in 1963 when his deep gospel/blues song 'If You Need Me' made the US Top 75 for the small American independent label Double L.

The song made such an impression with Atlantic Records producer Jerry Wexler that he covered it with Solomon Burke, who was already signed to the label, and it became a massive hit. It was through this that Jerry met Wilson Pickett himself and ultimately signed to Atlantic where he is best remembered for the classic 'In The Midnight Hour'.

POINTER SISTERS

The striking aspect of the four Pointer Sisters was always their incredible blend of harmony. Together with an individual image and a commerciality to their music they became what is essentially the En Vogue of the late

Seventies and early Eighties—lending amazing voices that came from the roots of soul to songs that best suited the pop idiom.

Ruth, Anitá, June and Bonnie come from Oakland, California, and were the daughters of church ministers. Bonnie and June first worked together in a youth choir before Anita and Ruth joined them in the early Seventies. They then perfected a stage and cabaret act which they took to San Francisco.

Not a typical soul group, the Pointer sisters enjoyed mainstream success on the strength of outstanding vocal harmonies and well-crafted pop songs.

Their vocal harmonies soon impressed artists like Elvin Bishop, Esther Phillips, Taj Mahal and Boz Scaggs, who utilized them on recording projects and live tours before the release of their own album *The Pointer Sisters* in 1973. What brought them particular attention at the start of their own career were their Forties dress and the nostalgic elements in their music style which immediately gave them an appeal outside black music.

PRINCE

Prince, born Prince Rogers Nelson in north Minneapolis in 1958, is without question the most recognized genius in the whole history of black music, drawing from many modern and traditional music forms, fusing them together and breaking the rules in the most inspired ways. This makes it difficult to get a true identity of who he is because he never reflects a one-dimensional character.

His voice and image combine male and female sexuality, crossing boundary lines. Overall he is revolutionary in the same way that Madonna makes people think and challenge the stereotypical attitudes of our time. If perhaps in a tongue-in-cheek pop idiom, and often very controversial, Prince has been moving music forward, establishing new ground for rhythms and arrangements, but taking soul music into areas that most other artists couldn't even imagine, let alone create.

A fountain of inspiration, Prince has written and produced an incredible amount of music for other artists too and after more than 10 years shows no sign that he has run dry of ideas. He is also important in that he began his career at a time when black soul and white rock audiences were particularly segregated and was influential in bringing them much closer together—in much the same way that Sly And The Family Stone had tried to do a decade before.

If Prince never recorded another song, he could release a 14-track album of unreleased product every year until 2028!

OTIS REDDING

See separate entry in the Legends section.

LIONEL RICHIE

Commercially, Lionel Richie is one of the most successful singer/songwriters in black music history. Creatively he was more innovative during his day as leader of the Commodores, but as a solo balladeer from the late Seventies onwards he perfected a formula which appealed equally to black and white audiences, in fact a very acceptable style to suit both in soul and pop music idioms. Vocally he expresses his own work extremely well, although he is unlikely to be remembered as one of soul music's true greats. However he will always be recognized for his immense success.

He was born in Tuskegee, Alabama, in 1949, and formed the Commodores with musician friends at university. He remained with the funk group for 15 years, first exploring his skills as a balladeer in 1977 with 'Easy', the group's first UK hit.

As a songwriter/producer, he also managed hits for Kenny Rogers ('Lady'), Diana Ross ('Missing You'), USA For Africa ('We Are The World', co-written with Michael Jackson), and his duet with Diana Ross, 'Endless Love'. One of the last heavyweight artists to record for Motown, he recently changed labels to Mercury.

MINNIE RIPERTON

One of the saddest losses to black music and music in general, Minnie Riperton possessed one of the most pure, sensitive, emotional and beautiful voices heard to date. With her five and a half-octave range, in clarity of tone, expression and communication she had the finest balance of all vocal qualities and attributes. Her voice encompassed a combination of all the finest and essential elements to be found in the all-round singer.

Although clearly influenced by the black music of her time, she also drew from many other musical forms. She aspired in her work to develop and encourage positiveness in others, and even while aware of her own tragic life circumstances, she did not want to focus her work in the melancholic but in the wonderment of life. She has influenced modern artists such as Kate Bush and others, as well as numerous fellow black artists.

She was born in Chicago in 1947 and intended to become an opera singer before her work with a local group took her to a career as a soul singer. She is best remembered for her hit 'Loving You' (1975).

SMOKEY ROBINSON

See separate entry in the Legends section.

DIANA ROSS

See separate entry in the Legends section.

ROSE ROYCE

Rose Royce came from the classic era of Seventies American black music, their music accompanying the film which reflected the images, dialogue and sounds of this time—Car Wash. With their original lead singer Gwen Dickey, they also had an accomplished vocalist who took already well crafted songs like 'Wishing On A Star' and 'Love Don't Live Here Anymore' and made them soul classics which remain popular to this day.

They formed in Los Angeles during the early Seventies and worked originally under the name Total Concept Unlimited as a backing group to Motown artist Edwin Starr. The line up was originally Kenny Copeland (lead vocal/trumpet), Michael Moore (sax), Freddie Dunn (trumpet), Lequeint "Duke" Jobe (bass/vocals), Walter McKinney (guitar), Michael Nash (keyboards), Terral Santiel (percussion), and Henry Garner (drums/vocals). In 1973 they met Motown producer Norman Whitfield (responsible for the Temptations' 'Papa Was A Rolling Stone' and other classics), who put them together with Gwen Dickey and changed their name to Rose Royce.

DAVID RUFFIN

JIMMY RUFFIN

David Ruffin was one of the greatest soul voices of the Sixties, even though his solo career was short-lived and relatively unsuccessful. He was, however, the leader of the Temptations during their Sixties heyday and possessed a voice that was versatile (from the grittily intense to the silky smooth), technically exceptional and ultimately soulful with its convincing, emotional expression. His work with the Temptations often verged on being solo performances, but his desire to be centre of attention was his undoing. When Motown wouldn't rename the group "David Ruffin And The Temptations" (as in Diana Ross And The Supremes), his departure, coupled with a drug addiction, led to his eventual downfall.

He was born in Meridian, Mississippi, in 1941, but moved to Detroit in 1960 where he first joined the Temptations as their drummer. Becoming lead singer he took the group to international stardom with 'My Girl', 'Since I Lost My Baby', 'Ain't Too Proud To Beg', and 'Beauty Is Only Skin Deep'. Motown didn't want to remove him from the group, but they wouldn't change the name either, so in 1968 he left to pursue a solo career.

Ironically, his début solo release 'My Whole World Ended (The Moment You Left Me)' couldn't have been more appropriate. Although he continued to record consistently through to 1980, his only solo success was 'Walk Away From Love' in 1974.

Jimmy Ruffin will always be best remembered for his first hit 'What Becomes Of The Broken Hearted', a truly great soul classic which is the closest Motown producers Mickey Stevenson and William Weatherspoon came to imitating the mighty Holland, Dozier and Holland and the one record which prevents Jimmy from being totally overshadowed artistically by brother David Ruffin, who became lead singer with the Temptations.

Jimmy was born in Colinsville, Mississippi, in 1939, but moved to Detroit in 1960 where he signed to Motown in 1964. The Temptations offered the position of lead singer to Jimmy before David, but choosing to stay solo he recorded a string of releases which were particularly successful in the UK, prompting his move to London. His main contribution in the Seventies was 'Tell Me What You Want', a single issued by Polydor which was claimed by many as one of the first true disco records when released in 1974.

RUFUS

Rufus were a masterful group, crafted by exceptional musicianship and vibrant both live and on record. By fusing black soul and white rock with such a seamless link they created a unique new style of music and were definitely the most inspired group of their generation. This,

Jimmy Ruffin achieved major success with the great soul classic 'What Becomes Of The Broken Hearted' in 1966.

coupled with the brilliance and freshness of the new voice of soul, Chaka Khan, made them a group to be reckoned with alongside any band in any music of their time.

The group first formed in Chicago in 1970 with vocalist Paulette McWilliams. When Chaka Khan came on board in 1973, the line-up settled as Chaka Khan (vocals), Al Ciner (vocals/guitar—later Tony Maiden), Andre Fisher (drums—later John Robinson), Kevin Murphy (keyboards), Bobby Watson (bass), David "Hawk" Wolinski (keyboards), and David Williams (guitar).

Recording consistently through the Seventies, they avoided the trendy disco and Philly idioms of black music, stayed with what they did best and released a legacy of exceptional music.

SADE

Sade has managed to establish a place for herself which no other black singer has as yet challenged. She stands alone with her unusual non-vibrato, non-tremolo, pure-toned, seductive yet often melancholic vocal style in which she fuses modern atmospheric, almost new music with cocktail jazzy elements. There were some who heralded her as an Eighties Billie Holiday, although they have different voices. Sade's is haunting with its touching quality which she adapts to be poignant with a balance of commerciality.

She also possesses a unique image, very cool, non-showbusiness and classy, her own name also being the

Sade, who has been heralded as an Eighties Billie Holiday, has a haunting, seductive and slightly melancholy vocal style.

official name for her group who write, play and produce all the songs.

She was born Helen Folasade Adu in Ibada, Nigeria, in 1959, but as a young child moved to London where she took up a career designing menswear before joining a north London group, Pride, and ultimately forming Sade in 1984. She manages to combine her love of writing and poetry with sensitive productions containing a balance of commercialism and artistry—if perhaps she doesn't have the greatest vocal range.

SAM AND DAVE

Sam And Dave perfectly captured the essence of what the Stax sound was all about in the mid-Sixties, 'Soul Man' being the duo's best remembered song commercially although a great deal more of their work charted and was critically acclaimed.

It is a well-known fact that as individuals Sam Moore (from Florida) and Dave Prater (from Georgia) could not stand each other, but their vocal harmonies were second to none and often their fight for space on recordings led to extra-dynamic performances—although Sam most definitely was the better singer.

They first sang together in 1958 before they became a premier act at Stax and worked with their best writers and producers. By the mid-Sixties they had established themselves as soul stars on both sides of the Atlantic with hits including 'Soul Man'. The demise of Stax and the arrival of funk and disco in the Seventies led directly to the split of Sam And Dave at the end of a golden era for southern-based soul.

SHALAMAR

When Los Angeles jumped on the disco band wagon of the Seventies, Dick Griffey launched a label called Soul Train and put together a group of regular dancers from the *Soul Train* TV show that was filmed for broadcast in the city. He called the group Shalamar, and their début release 'Uptown Festival' became a major hit in 1977.

When Soul Train records underwent a name change to Solar Records the following year, Shalamar became officially Howard Hewett, Jody Watley and Jeffrey Daniel and, with the help of producer Leon Sylvers, they went on to epitomize the individual Solar sound which held its own on the dancefloor between the late Seventies and early Eighties.

Groups like Dynasty, Lakeside, the Whispers and Midnight Star all came from the same school and all had success with the sound, but Shalamar took it to its greatest heights with such hits as 'Take That To The Bank', 'The Second Time Around' and 'A Night To Remember'. When dance music trends began to change, Shalamar survived briefly by adopting a more mainstream style, but all original members now have solo careers.

SISTER SLEDGE

Sister Sledge have been making records from the early Seventies through to this day, but they are unlikely to surpass the excellence of their work with writers/producers Nile Rodgers and Bernard Edwards at the height of the disco era. Songs such as 'We Are Family', 'He's The Greatest Dancer', and 'Lost In Music' have to date proved to be timeless, appealing to every new generation of soul and dance fans.

'Lost In Music' could probably be a hit every 5 years!

Debbie, Joni, Kathy and Kim Sledge from Philadelphia initially sang gospel, and later did backgrounds for producers Gamble and Huff, but landed at the right place at the right time when signed by Atlantic Records. Nile Rodgers and Bernard Edwards had been perfecting a unique new dance production style with their own group Chic and, through being signed to the same record label, were brought in to utilize their infectious mix of strings, rhythm guitar and dance grooves on what became a series of Seventies classics.

SLY AND THE FAMILY STONE

Sly And The Family Stone was the brainchild of a former Californian DJ Sylvester Stewart, born in Dallas, Texas, in 1944. From playing the psychedelic rock and soul music of the day back to back on his radio show, Sylvester went one step further by forming his own group and integrating the two music forms together to create "psychedelic soul". So perfect was the marriage of these two quite different music styles that he brought the two audiences the closest they've ever been and was a major influence on many artists that followed, including Prince.

Sly And The Family Stone was not only about bringing music forms together; Sylvester "Sly" Stewart also had a vision of bringing people of all races and backgrounds together. His downfall was his addiction to cocaine, which in time made him less attuned to the outside world and more introverted. At times he would fail to turn up at his own concerts, but it was a long time before the drugs impaired his ability to make at least a good dance groove (if perhaps not an inspired lyric).

SOUL II SOUL

Although Soul II Soul have to be heralded as being the most important black group to emerge in the history of black music in the late Eighties, they have unfortunately failed to maintain their credibility as serious black music makers. With their constant change of vocalists, none being as interesting or equally talented as Caron Wheeler (who brought them initial success), Soul II Soul have lost a great deal of their inspired start.

Prior to being a recording enterprise, Soul II Soul was a touring troupe of DJs and rappers under the guidance of their leader Beresford "Jazzy B" Romeo from south London. A move into making records was inevitable and Jazzy recruited Nellee Hooper, the musician who was instrumental in shaping the shuffling Soul II Soul sound, a highly infectious, danceable mid-tempo two-step rhythm which not only swept the UK as a much needed breather from house music, but engrossed the US black music scene for a couple of years.

Although their début release *Fairplay* (featuring vocalist Rose Windross) got critical acclaim, their sound wasn't yet defined and it was with Caron Wheeler's voice firmly in place that *Keep On Movin'* took the world by storm in 1989, swiftly followed by *Back To Life*.

LISA STANSFIELD

While Cilla Black and Dusty Springfield were considered to be the white soul singers of the Sixties, Lisa Stansfield from Rochdale, Lancashire, in some ways represents a Nineties equivalent. She's from a show-business background, down to earth, although more inspired than both

as she at least co-writes and sings her own material. Cilla and Dusty both sang songs that established the careers of both Aretha Franklin and Dionne Warwick in America, while Lisa co-writes and produces material for both herself and Dionne Warwick, incidentally!

As with Dusty Springfield, who was actually signed to Motown in the Sixties, Lisa clearly wants to be recognized as a serious singer comparable with the legends of black soul music. This to an extent she has achieved, albeit her success to date being placed more in a pop soul form rather than the classic soul expression of her great black counterparts. Whether Lisa will ever achieve a position among the greats is yet to be seen, but she is certainly one of the UK's finest singers and has at least two near classics to her name with 'Big Thing' (with her group Blue Zone) and 'All Around The World'.

Lisa Stansfield: one of the few white British singers recognized on the international soul scene.

THE STYLISTICS

As their name would imply, the Stylistics personified the smooth and silky-styled vocal groups of the Seventies. Their particular success was rooted in the perfect marriage of Russell Thomkins's soulful, innocent falsetto lead vocals, the romantic lyrics of Linda Creed and the sensitive, emotion-induced arrangements and productions of Thom Bell. At face value, the Stylistics often ran the risk of being corny with much of their music, but in a sense that was the commercial element that made them so successful. They introduced the Philly sound to the world.

Russell Thomkins, Aaron Love, James Smith, Herbie Murrell and James Dunn formed the Stylistics in Philadelphia in 1968, and when they signed to Avco in 1971, it was at a time when the Philly sound was preparing itself to take over from Sixties Motown to become the most prominent sound in black music during the Seventies. Thom Bell and the team of Kenny Gamble and Leon Huff were all key players during this transition, but while Gamble and Huff played heavily on rhythms and a big sound, Thom Bell utilized Philly orchestrations in a more laid-back and sensitive way for his work with groups such as the Delphonics, the Detroit Spinners and, the most successful of them all, the Stylistics.

With songs like 'I'm Stone In Love With You', the Stylistics were the commercial face of Philly soul in the Seventies.

DONNA SUMMER

Born Adrian Donna Gaines in Boston, Massachusetts, in 1948, Donna Summer was dubbed "the Queen of Disco" in the Seventies and is one of the few artists from that genre to survive and maintain a successful career through to this day. The key to her long-term success has been her exceptional voice, which she has always been able to adapt to the commercial dance music of the day. Her initial success, meanwhile, came from her ability to cross disco to the mainstream masses.

Doing away with the lavish orchestrations and acoustic rhythm sections that were the backbone of disco, her producers Moroder and Bellotte devised an electronic sound created by synthesizers. It was a fresh sound that marked the transition between Seventies disco and Eighties high energy.

Vocally, Donna is not a typical soul singer; she has a distinctive pure-toned, clean-sounding voice which is spiritual more than emotional but with a beauty and honesty which places her in a position of her own. What was unusual was that the purity in her voice was married to challenging, confrontational and *risqué* material that was not so pure at all, although after disco died she proved to be a more serious singer.

THE SUPREMES

The story of the Supremes is one of rags to riches whereby three poor girls from Detroit's ghetto became the most popular female vocal group of all time. This was, at least, until the departure of their original lead singer in the late Sixties although it can't be argued that her replacement, Jean Terrell, did give the group some memorable moments through the early Seventies.

It was Smokey Robinson who gave Diana Ross, Mary Wilson and Florence Ballard a break at Motown Records in Detroit (poaching the group's guitarist Marv Tarplin in the process), but it was Holland, Dozier and Holland who generated all their hits in a style that became known as the Motown sound. Their hits, including 'Where Did Our Love Go', 'Baby Love' and 'Stop In The Name Of Love', became the sound of young America and later catapulted Diana Ross to solo stardom.

When Jean Terrell took over in 1970, the group enjoyed half a dozen more hits, but with their loss of Diana and Motown's loss of Holland, Dozier and Holland it was essentially the end of an era for a group that so typified the Motown sound.

KEITH SWEAT

The arrival of Keith Sweat's solo career in 1987 coincided with the time that producer Teddy Riley was pioneering a new production style to become known as new jack swing (or swing beat).

When Teddy Riley produced Keith's *Make It Last Forever* album in 1987, songs like 'I Want Her', 'Something Just Ain't Right', and 'Don't Stop Your Love' were among the first to be produced in this style, and while Keith wallowed in the emotional sentiment of each song, the album established both a singer of great potential and a producer who then took his style to further success with his own group Guy and a new generation of soul groups and singers.

Born in Harlem, New York, Keith "Sabu" Crier formed a group Sabu And The Survivors before becoming a key player with jazz fusion innovators Rhythm Makers and later G.Q., who scored success with songs like 'Disco Nights—Rock Freak' during the late Seventies and early Eighties. More recently he has also been responsible for producing the group Silk.

SYLVESTER

Sylvester was a revolutionary singer of his time, standing out as an artist not just in terms of his music, but also for his unusual outward image and persona. He was important for his musical contributions as well as for challenging

With songs like 'I Want Her', Keith Sweat with producer Teddy Riley kick-started the swing beat sound of the late Eighties/early Nineties.

stereotypes with his very common use of cross-dressing and flamboyancy, equally accepted by both his gay and straight audiences. He was responsible, too, for carving the careers of his backing singers Martha Wash and Izora Armstead.

He was born Sylvester James in Los Angeles in 1946, and was a child gospel star before he moved to San Francisco. With disco at its peak, Sylvester fully embraced both the gay lifestyle from where disco was born and the music itself and delivered in 1978 'You Make Me Feel (Mighty Real)', a record that laid a foundation for the high-energy music which was soon to follow with the advent of a more electronic, less acoustic production style.

There was a much more sensitive side to Sylvester's music which came through on songs like 'Here Is My Love', his duet with Jeanie Tracy, and his songwriting for Martha and Izora, although this was largely overshadowed by his larger-than-life prominence on the dance scene, particularly with gay audiences.

THE TEMPTATIONS

See separate entry in the Legends section.

* * *

THE THREE DEGREES

The Three Degrees were the most successful of all the Philadelphia girl groups in the Seventies, their success being engineered by writers/producers Kenny Gamble and Leon Huff and their Philadelphia International hit-making machine. Vocally the voluptuous, seductive and sensual lead singer Sheila Ferguson was a contributory factor for the group's immense popularity on songs like 'When Will I See You Again' and, considering there had been so many girl trios through the Sixties had left such a weight of successful material, one must only respect the Three Degrees for managing to make such a mark with their music through the Seventies and early Eighties.

The original Three Degrees were Fayette Pinkney, Shirley Porter and Linda Turner before producer Richard Barrett amended the group to Fayette with Sheila Ferguson and Valerie Thompson in 1966.

They were first utilized at Philadelphia International to feature on MFSB's US Number 1 smash 'TSOP' (The Sound of Philadelphia) which in 1974 celebrated the sound which was then the most powerful force in black music since the demise of the Motown sound. The song was also used as the theme tune to the legendary US music TV programme *Soul Train*.

* * *

IKE AND TINA TURNER

Ike Turner from Clarksdale, Mississippi, (born in 1931) married Tina Turner from Brownsville, Tennessee, (born Anna Mae Bullock in 1938) in 1958 and from 1960 The Ike And Tina Turner Revue became legendary on the live circuit with a dazzling stage show built on Tina's dynamic vocals.

When the Revue disbanded in 1974, Tina established a major solo career exactly 10 years later by placing herself in a unique musical position. Unusual among black artists, Tina incorporates a lot of rock elements in her singing, fusing white rock with black R&B in her music. However, while vocally Tina relies not so much on the smooth, melodic silky approach more common in soul singers, she delivers songs with such a heartfelt outward conviction that one can not deny her contribution in soul terms. She has to be recognized as being one of the most hard-working, giving and respected black female singers from the Sixties onwards.

Ike and Tina Turner first recorded together in 1960 although they are best remembered for a much later track, 'Nutbush City Limits' (1973). They divorced in 1976, and it was only in 1983 that Tina picked up her career to become one of the most successful solo recording artists of the Eighties with songs including 'Let's Stay Together' and 'What's Love Got To Do With It'. She continues to record and perform with consistent excellence despite several farewell tours!

Silky, silky soul: Luther Vandross epitomizes the sophisticated modern soul balladeer. All his albums are multi-platinum in the US.

LUTHER VANDROSS

Luther Vandross has to be the balladeer of all balladeers in modern soul music. With the smoothest, silkiest of tones Luther is an inspired singer with an agile voice over which he has full command and control. He may not necessarily have the most expressive voice emotionally, but he has a beautiful tone and is the supreme master of contemporary soul ballads.

He was born in the Bronx, New York, in 1951, and in the early Seventies wrote songs for the all-black version of *The Wiz*. He worked with David Bowie as a vocal arranger on the *Young Americans* album and by the mid-Seventies he was also a top session singer.

Luther's own recording career had begun in 1975, although it was only through his work as featured vocalist with Bionic Boogie ('Hot Butterfly') and Change ('Glow Of Love'/'Searchin'') that he became noticed on the soul scene. His solo career took off in 1981 after signing to Epic Records, and through producing all his own work he established a sophisticated style that brought not only his own success, but work for other artists including Aretha Franklin, Dionne Warwick and Diana Ross.

DIONNE WARWICK

. Dionne Warwick's career was carved from the writing and producing of Burt Bacharach and Hal David, two white men whose reputation had been built around their work with Fifties pop singers such as Perry Como and Tony Bennett.

While Dionne had previously sung in gospel groups, Bacharach and David realized her voice was particularly well suited to crossover music, and she became essentially a white person's black singer. Vocally you could say she is the female equivalent of a Johnny Mathis, distinctive in sound with quality of tone, but not possessing any uniqueness in ability. She is essentially a pop singer who appeals to a universal audience and has become a household name in a crossover music market through classic soft soul songs like 'Walk On By' and 'Anyone Who Had A Heart'.

She was born Marie Dionne Warwick in East Orange, New Jersey, in 1940, her musical family including cousin Cissy Houston (mother of Whitney Houston) and sister Dee Dee Warwick (also a recording artist). Recording through to this day, her appeal to R&B audiences has been aided by the productions of Holland, Dozier and Holland, Thom Bell, Jay Graydon, Luther Vandross, Stevie Wonder and Lisa Stansfield.

THE WHISPERS

Vocal group the Whispers have consistently made great soul records since the early Seventies, but are perhaps best recognized for their contribution to the quality end of what was happening on the disco scene with songs such as 'And The Beat Goes On' and 'It's A Love Thing'.

The group were formed by Texas-born brothers Wallace and Walter Scott in the mid-Sixties after their move to Los Angeles, where they were joined by Nicholas Caldwell, Marcus Hutson and Gordy Hamilton. Gordy Hamilton was later replaced by Leaveil Degree. It is the super-smooth and often jazz-tinged vocals of Walter Scott, however, that has kept the group in business over so many years—not to belittle the contribution made by their great material and slick productions that never catered blatantly to pop audiences.

Through the early Seventies they imitated the Philly sound before Soul Train Records (later to become Solar Records) instigated their transition to West Coast disco. Later, with the help of producer Leon Sylvers, they typified the flavour of the time on the West Coast dance scene before they conceived the idea in 1981 of dividing their albums into upbeat (dance) and downbeat (ballads) sides, which lasted until the intervention of the CD.

BARRY WHITE

Barry White is unusual in that he is a bass singer, whereas most other successful soul singers are tenors. Furthermore, as a singer he may not be as respected as the soul greats like Marvin Gaye and Otis Redding, but he was more successful than any of them. This success was down to the perfect marriage of his deep voice with big orchestrations, tight rhythms and commercial songs that were invariably based on love and sex—which, while common, he played on to such a degree they became almost an overstatement. It was a sound which didn't belong to any school, unusual in that he used huge orchestration rather than the group or band which

Karyn White (see page 94) is married to one of soul music's most successful songwriter/producers, Babyface.

accompanied most singers, and in his heyday Barry stood alone as being one of the most successful black artists in commercial music. He became the big daddy of black love singers, influencing a new generation of singers and production styles for the Seventies and Eighties.

He was born in Galveston, Texas, in 1944 but grew up in Los Angeles where he began his professional music career as an arranger and then producer for Bob And Earl (best remembered for 'Harlem Shuffle' in 1963).

KARYN WHITE

Karyn White is a relatively new solo singer on the soul scene, but has a career as an in-demand session singer that goes back to the early Eighties.

She was born in Los Angeles and toured as a backing singer with O'Bryan before fusion keyboard instrumentalist Jeff Lorber utilized her as featured vocalist on his 1986 dance hit 'Facts Of Love'. Through this affiliation she signed directly to Warner Brothers as a solo artist where she worked with in-vogue writers/producers L.A. and Babyface on a platinum-selling début album which featured the hits 'The Way You Love Me', 'Superwoman' and 'Secret Rendezvous'.

She is now married to the album's co-producer Babyface, and is likely to become one of the major soul recording artists of the Nineties.

DENIECE WILLIAMS

Deniece Williams is one of the most beautiful, truly inspirational and amazing vocalists of her generation and in the history of black music. With her delicately powerful, pure and charmingly sweet voice, Deniece has to be recognized for her brilliance and uniqueness in her unusual marriage of soul, gospel, funk, classical and even opera among her great breadth of musical accomplishment. Furthermore, regardless of her four-octave range, beauty of sound, perfect pitch and bird-like agility in her voice, Deniece never allows technicality to overshadow her truly soulful expression, and aside from her commitment to black music, she also has respect on a pop level.

Born June Deniece Chandler in Gary, Indiana, in 1951, she grew up on a gospel diet but was inspired by the secular music of the day, and after Stevie Wonder heard her single 'Love Is Tears' she joined his group Wonderlove.

Her solo career took off in 1976 when Maurice White of Earth Wind And Fire heard her demos and signed her to Columbia Records where her hits included 'Free', 'That's What Friends Are For', 'Baby Baby, My Love Is All For You', 'Too Much, Too Little, Too Late' with Johnny Mathis and 'Let's Hear It For The Boy'.

Deniece Williams has one of the most critically acclaimed voices but has had most of her success with commercial pop music.

BILL WITHERS

Bill Withers was the voice on the Grammy award-winning song 'Just The Two Of Us', but he is best recognized for his outstanding songwriting, most notably with 'Ain't No Sunshine', 'Lean On Me' and 'Lovely Day'. A self-taught musician, Bill's music has always had a fairly broad appeal, while his writing too over the years has tackled a wide range of issues such as politics, equality and, like most soul artists, matters of the heart!

He was born in Slab Fork, West Virginia, in 1938, and first recorded with producer Booker T. Jones for Sussex Records in the early Seventies. It was his first album *Just As I Am* that featured his song 'Ain't No Sunshine' which was later to be a solo hit for Michael Jackson (and has been covered by numerous artists over the years).

He did not write a great many songs through the Seventies, but when he did they were worth hearing and were recorded by such major artists as Aretha Franklin ('Let Me In Your Life') and Diana Ross ('The Same Love That Made Me Laugh'). He recorded his biggest and best-remembered solo hit 'Lovely Day' in 1978.

WOMACK AND WOMACK

Womack And Womack are Los Angeles-based husband and wife Cecil and Linda Womack, Linda being the daughter of the legendary Sam Cooke, and Cecil the brother of Bobby Womack. As Womack And Womack, Cecil and Linda present an earthier form of soul less common in black music these days, their sound fusing more acoustic styles with elements of folk music. Down to earth in its presentation, their music is a strong appreciation of black and white forms merged together with Linda's voice so well suited as it is so untypically black.

The songwriting collaboration of Womack And Womack began in the mid Sixties, at a time when Linda had already established songwriting credentials by penning 'I'm In Love' for Wilson Pickett and the James Taylor/Bobby Womack duet 'A Woman's Gotta Have It'. Together they are best recognized for 'Love TKO', a song they penned for Teddy Pendergrass that they later recorded themselves.

Their greatest commercial success came in 1988 with their UK hits 'Teardrops', and 'Life Is Just A Ballgame', although they have yet to be successful in the US. They currently record for WEA.

BOBBY WOMACK

While Bobby Womack comes from the tradition of deep-throated, intense and expressive soul vocalists of the Sixties, he is one of the few from that school who has survived through to the present day maintaining what is virtually a cult following.

He was born in Cleveland, Ohio, in 1944, and originally sang lead with his brothers' group the Valentinos.

While on tour they met Sam Cooke who signed them to his Sar label and also employed Bobby as his guitarist. He subsequently went to play guitar for Aretha Franklin, Ray Charles and many more before Sam Cooke's death prompted him to pursue a solo career.

Through the late Sixties he recorded for numerous small labels before in 1971 settling with United Artists where he recorded such soul gems as 'Harry Hippie' and 'You're Welcome', 'Stop On By', among his several albums through to 1975. What he suffered most from was lack of major chart success, a situation which didn't improve at Columbia where he recorded until 1978.

In 1979 producer Patrick Moten engineered a sound he later applied to Anita Baker's milestone album *The Songstress*, but on Bobby's Arista album *Roads Of Life*, and subsequent *Poet 1* and *Poet 2* albums for the Beverly Glen label, incredible music ruled over chart activity.

STEVIE WONDER

See separate entry in the Legends section.

✳ ✳ ✳

Womack And Womack, steeped in soul music tradition and a force in popular music.

legends

JAMES BROWN

The Godfather of Soul

* * *

Singer/Songwriter
Born: 1932, Barnwell, South Carolina, USA

JAMES BROWN IS WITHOUT DOUBT ONE OF THE MOST INFLUENTIAL ARTISTS IN BLACK MUSIC AND IS DESERVEDLY RECOGNIZED AS "THE GODFATHER OF SOUL". HIS CAREER NOW SPANS VIRTUALLY 40 YEARS AND HIS MUSIC HAS NOW INSPIRED MANY GENERATIONS OF ARTISTS AS WELL AS NEW MUSIC FORMS.

He succeeded by breaking down the musical conventions of the Forties and Fifties and coupled his dynamic, energetic and flamboyant personality with an insatiable desire to reach the top. Vocally he did not have the beauty of voice, the traditional gospel-derived phrasing and sensitivity of other greats such as Sam Cooke, Otis Redding or Marvin Gaye—in fact his voice was throaty and ragged. Instead he demolished convention by immersing intense expression and often sexual passion in uncharted rhythmical waters and a musical frenzy of percussion and blaring horns.

He was born in South Carolina in 1932, but was raised by his aunt in Augusta, Georgia. During his teens he formed a gospel group, the 3 Swanees, with Bobby Byrd and Johnny Terry and relocated to Macon, Georgia, where Little Richard and the Five Royals were already enjoying success. It was Little Richard's manager Clint Brantley who first recognized the potential of James and his friends in 1956. Clint organized the recording of 'Please Please Please' which landed James and his group—now called the Famous Flames—a record deal with the Federal label (a subsidiary of King).

The record may only have scraped into the US Top 100, but it launched the greatest individual career in the history of R&B. He

James Brown was crowned "the Godfather of Soul" and was a pioneer of the Seventies funk movement.

nearly lost his record deal by delivering nine unsuccessful follow-ups, but with the release of 'Try Me (I Need You)' in 1958 began the first of 12 consecutive hits to 1960.

His songs during the Fifties did not have the clear individuality of his later work, but it did showcase his potential to booking agent Ben Bart who gave James the opportunity to expand his group the Flames to 20 members and upwards and promote what was to become the legendary James Brown Revue.

Through the Sixties and Seventies James Brown became the hardest working man in show business, using the versatility and benefits of a well-rehearsed band to experiment and also punctuate the vocal interplay between himself and his group. When all this was capsulated live at a recording of his show at the Apollo Theatre in New York in 1962 James became a major star.

His success was consolidated in 1963 when 'Prisoner Of Love' became both his first US Top 20 hit and influential in recognizing James's own new style. It was part derived

from elements of dance hall music of the Fifties (from where elements of his sound came from), but essentially it presented a whole new way of ballad singing. It was radical in that a pop standard was made to sound so intensely personal.

Had he not the means to start his own production company, James's creativity could have been stifled in the mid Sixties by the conservatism of his record company, King. But with independence, James was able to fund recordings which he took to Smash Records in Chicago. However, after the release of 'Out Of Sight' for that label in 1964, a legal wrangle brought him back to King, this time with full control of his destiny.

The first release under this new arrangement was 'Papa's Got A Brand New Bag' on which the James Brown sound truly arrived, in a totally innovative record bursting with new rhythms and powerhouse brass and screaming vocals.

The follow-up was James's biggest American hit, 1966's 'I Got You (I Feel Good)'. In 1967 he was again innovative with the release of 'Cold Sweat', a funky grove of irregular structure that relentlessly ploughed away and pointed to where he and the likes of Sly Stone were to take funk in the Seventies.

In between he had recorded 'Say It Loud, I'm Black And I'm Proud' in response to the American street riots of 1968, and found himself on a delicate political soap box which almost cost him his music career, but in 1970 he bounced back with his greatest record 'Get Up I Feel Like Being A Sex Machine' (1970). The record, along with 'Funky Drummer' (with its drum loop countlessly copied in modern day soul/hip-hop) helped kick-start the whole Seventies funk era. The Seventies was also James's most commercially successful period with hits such as 'Hey America' and 'Soul Power'.

Through the Eighties he recorded for a number of labels such as TK, Scotti Brothers and Augusta Sound and after becoming the "most sampled" artist on the rap/hip-hop scene remained with Scotti Brothers for the album *I'm Real* (1988).

THE FOUR TOPS

The Indestructible Soul Quartet!

* * *

Levi Stubbs—born c. 1938, Detroit, Michigan, USA
Renaldo Benson—born 1947, Detroit, Michigan, USA
Lawrence Payton—born c. 1938, Detroit, Michigan, USA
Abdul Fakir—born c. 1938, Detroit, Michigan, USA

*T*HE FOUR TOPS ARE LEVI STUBBS, RENALDO "OBIE" BENSON, LAWRENCE PAYTON AND ABDUL "DUKE" FAKIR. THEY ARE A VOCAL GROUP WHO HAVE SURVIVED 40 YEARS OF CHANGE AND REMAIN ONE OF THE MOST POPULAR GROUPS ON THE SOUL SCENE TODAY.

With the help of legendary Motown writers/producers Holland, Dozier and Holland they made some of the most memorable recordings of the Sixties and were one of the few American black acts to compete on a grand scale with the Beatles during this time.

The guys met in high school in Detroit and first sang together as the Aims. From the mid Fifties through to the early Sixties they perfected a nightclub act which ultimately lead to a recording contract with Motown in 1963. The group were signed as a result of sheer hard work rather than a gospel upbringing or a lucky break, but it was the immense presence and strength of their lead vocalist Levi Stubbs, Jackie Wilson's cousin, that gave them their first American hit with 'Baby I Need Your Loving'.

The combination of Levi Stubbs, the vocal precision of Obie, Lawrence and Duke, the magic of Holland, Dozier and Holland and the might of the Motown organization produced mid-Sixties hits like 'I Can't Help Myself',

'It's The Same Old Song', 'Loving You Is Sweeter Than Ever', 'Reach Out I'll Be There', 'Standing In The Shadows Of Love' and 'Bernadette', which will last forever.

Their success with Motown continued through the early Seventies with less memorable hits, but in 1972 they turned to the ABC/ Dunhill label (Probe in the UK). Here they had success with 'Keeper Of The Castle' and 'Sweet Understanding Love' in 1973, but essentially it was their extremely well-polished live shows that maintained their popularity through the funk and disco-dominated Seventies.

Occasionally people wondered whether Levi would leave the group to embark on a solo career. In fact, Levi never did consider leaving; he and the group were brothers, a family, who in the title of their 1988 album, were *Indestructible*.

With another change of label to Casablanca in 1981 the Four Tops hit the top again with songs from the *Tonight* album such as 'When She Was My Girl' and 'Don't Walk Away'. But they were soon to return to Motown for the *Back Where I Belong* reunion album with Holland, Dozier and Holland. How the group could think they could recapture what they had in the Sixties with this combination

Motown legends the Four Tops in casual mode.

is hard to say. The Motown sound of the Sixties had died with the advent of looser music forms, advances in technology and the initial split of Holland, Dozier and Holland. Furthermore Motown's founder Berry Gordy had become more interested in film production. However, the group also made *Magic* and *Hot Nights* on Motown and a remixed 'Reach Out I'll Be There' was a Motown hit again in 1988.

The Four Tops are presently signed with Arista Records under the guidance of Clive Davis, discoverer of Whitney Houston and supervisor of soul legends Aretha Franklin and Dionne Warwick among others. Teaming the Four Tops up with Phil Collins and Holland, Dozier and Holland's Lamont Dozier partly recaptured the Motown sound and sold it to a contemporary audience on the song 'Loco In Acapulco' (1988) which remains the group's last hit. The Four Tops, however, are bound to bounce back. They continue to fill huge arenas, both independently and as part of the "Giants Of Motown" revues.

ARETHA FRANKLIN

The Queen of Soul

* * *

Singer/Songwriter/Keyboards/Producer
Born: 1942, Memphis, Tennessee, USA

*A*RETHA HAS TO BE WITHOUT DOUBT THE MOST EXCITING BLACK FEMALE SINGER TO EMERGE IN THE SIXTIES. CROSSING OVER THE TRUEST GOSPEL TRADITION OF SINGING INTO SOUL AND POP IDIOMS, SHE HAS TO BE THE MOST IMPORTANT, IDENTIFIABLE AND INFLUENTIAL FEMALE VOICE IN BLACK MUSIC. SHE HAS NOW INSPIRED SINGERS FOR THREE DECADES.

Aretha was born in Memphis, Tennessee, in 1942, one of four children and the second daughter of Baptist minister Rev. C. L. Franklin. She was already a legend by the time she was 14, singing in her father's church, but it was secular rather than gospel music that took her to the small JVP label in Detroit where her first recordings were made.

In 1960 she was signed by Columbia (CBS) Records where she worked with John Hammond, a former producer of Billie Holiday, on her first single for the label, 'Today I Sing The Blues', a US Top 10 R&B hit, prior to the release of her début album *Aretha* in 1961.

Aretha remained with Columbia for six years during which she moved to New York, married her manager Ted White and was crowned "the Queen of Soul". Her albums emulated popular female singers of the day (such as

From gospel roots, Aretha Franklin epitomizes the classic soul singer both on record and in concert.

Dionne Warwick on 'Walk On By'), and balanced her gospel vocals with pop jazz arrangements which were underrated and went without a great deal of commercial success. Clearly, had Aretha not had the experience that these years gave her to mature, she would not have so readily able to step into the studio with the ease and proficiency she did when in 1967 she left Columbia, signed to Atlantic and set off back to Memphis in search of a hit. Here she teamed up with Atlantic producer Jerry Wexler and the musicians of Stax studios to embark on the most prolific period of her career. Within a couple of years at Atlantic she had already notched up five gold singles, the title track of her début album for the label, 'I Never Loved A Man (The Way I Loved You)', being her first million-seller. Further hits flowed through the late Sixties: 'Respect', 'Baby I Love You', 'Chain of Fools', 'Since You've Been Gone', 'Think' and 'I Say A Little Prayer'. Her career

relevant to the Seventies. With the help of her sister Carolyn (who had also written 'Ain't No Way' and sang numerous backgrounds for her) she delivered one of her greatest records, 'Angel' (1973), from her Quincy Jones-produced album *Hey Now Hey*. The record was

suffered temporarily after her divorce from Ted White, at which point she moved back home and spent more time in church than the recording studio.

Her early Seventies success continued with 'Don't Play That Song', 'Spanish Harlem', 'Bridge Over Troubled Waters' and 'Rock Steady', by which time Aretha had moved away from the Stax idiom to part-embrace funk but essentially pursue a fuller pop gospel style more

only surpassed commercially by the Stevie Wonder co-written 'Until You Come Back To Me (That's What I'm Gonna Do)', also released in 1973 and taken from the 1974 album *Let Me In Your Life*.

Through the remainder of her days at Atlantic, Aretha struggled to reach the commercial heights of her late Sixties and early Seventies releases, but her albums remain the source of some classic soul music from a soul legend.

Rather than allowing herself to brood over lack of success and then the shooting of her father, who was left in a coma for five years, Aretha picked herself up with a new record company (Arista) and album *Aretha* (1980) which put her back in the charts courtesy of 'What A Fool Believes'. Her success through the Eighties continued with hit songs like 'Love All The Hurt Away', a duet with George Benson, 'Freeway of Love', 'Another Night', 'Sisters Are Doin' It For Themselves', a duet with the Eurythmics, and her only UK Number 1 hit, 'I Knew You Were Waiting (For Me)', a duet with George Michael. The success of the latter led to a number of duets through the Eighties with artists Larry Graham, Elton John, Whitney Houston, James Brown and Levi Stubbs (of the Four Tops).

While her present works are still always eagerly received, they haven't quite managed to achieve the same respect as her initial works during the Sixties and Seventies, although this hasn't diminished her position as "the Queen of Soul".

MARVIN GAYE

The Lover Man of Soul

* * *

Singer/Songwriter/Drummer
Born: 1939, Washington, DC, USA
Died: 1984, Los Angeles, CA, USA

*D*URING THE SIXTIES MOTOWN RECORDS DISCOVERED MANY SOUL SUPERSTARS AND LEGENDS, BUT FROM THESE MARVIN GAYE WAS THE GREATEST SOUL SINGER. HE HAD A UNIQUE WAY OF TOUCHING THE SOULS OF HIS LISTENERS WITH A VOICE THAT CARESSED AND WAS OFTEN ANGUISHED, SOUL-SEARCHING AND SELF-ABSORBED. HE ALSO BROUGHT AN INTENSITY TO HIS MUSIC THAT REFLECTED HIS VOLATILE PERSONALITY AND TROUBLED PERSONAL LIFE.

He was born Marvin Pentz Gaye in Washington (1939), the son of a minister who shot and killed him after a quarrel in 1984. Marvin both sang in church and learnt piano and drums in order to pursue a career in the music business. In the mid-Fifties he sang with vocal groups the Rainbows and the Marquees before teaming up with Harvey Fuqua and becoming a singer with the Moonglows in 1959. Harvey was soon to be given an influential position at Motown in Detroit and hired Marvin to work at the organization as a session drummer.

In 1961 he released his own début single 'Let Your Conscience Be Your Guide', but it was his self-penned song 'Stubborn Kind Of Fella' the following year that first dented the charts in the United States and was his first UK release (on the Oriole label which released Motown titles prior to the label's own affiliation with a UK major).

He became particularly close to the Motown family in 1962 by marrying Anna Gordy, a sister of Motown founder Berry Gordy, for whom he wrote his next US hit 'Pride And Joy'. His first hit on both sides of the Atlantic was 'How Sweet It Is' in 1964.

Through the remainder of the Sixties Marvin developed the idea of recording in conjunction with another singer, initially with Mary Wells ('Once Upon A Time'), then Kim Weston ('It Takes Two'), but ultimately Tammi Terrell with whom he established the greatest vocal partnership of the Sixties. No one ever knew whether they became lovers, but in song there was often an incredible intimacy as if to prove that they were, such as on hit songs 'If I Could Build My Whole World Around You', 'Ain't Nothin' Like The Real Thing', 'You're All I

Motown soul legend Marvin Gaye, later shot by his father who claimed self-defence.

Need To Get By', 'You Ain't Livin' Till You're Livin', 'Good Lovin' Ain't Easy To Come By', and 'The Onion Song'.

In the meantime Marvin had recorded 'I Heard It Through The Grapevine', but as Gladys Knight And The Pips were riding high in the charts with the song, Marvin's version sat unreleased for over a year. When it finally came out in 1968, it became one of Motown's biggest sellers ever, hitting Number 1 on both sides of the Atlantic.

Tragedy struck in 1970 with the sudden death of Tammi Terrell from a brain tumour. It happened during one of Marvin and Tammi's shows in Cleveland, Ohio, and devastated Marvin to the point that he temporarily became a recluse.

When he returned to the studio in 1971 he came back with an album which virtually remodelled R&B. His *What's Going On* album completely broke with traditional Motown and with a brand new experimental sound created what was essentially a matrix for what R&B became in the Seventies.

His work continued through the early Seventies with albums *Trouble Man* (1972), a soundtrack, *Let's Get It On* (1973), *Diana And Marvin* (1974) with Diana Ross, and a live recording of his show at the Oakland Coliseum in 1974 which was his first live appearance since the death of Tammi Terrell.

The late Seventies were more unstable years in Marvin's career, his *I Want You* album (1976) critically acclaimed but lacking substantial hits, 'Got To Give It Up' giving him a huge hit single in 1977, but his painful divorce from Anna Gordy attracting publicity when he withheld royalties due to her from an album *Here My Dear* (1979), which he recorded to reflect his feelings about the situation.

After further drug and tax problems, he left America vowing never to record for Motown again and settled in Belgium. Here he was tracked down by a Columbia Records executive who, in 1982, signed him for a long-term recording deal. Tragically he was shot after the release of just one album, *Midnight Love*, which contained Marvin's last major hit 'Sexual Healing'.

THE ISLEY BROTHERS

The Ultimate Soul Survivors

* * *

Ronald Isley, singer—born 1941, Cincinatti, Ohio, USA
Rudolph Isley, singer—born 1939, Cincinatti, Ohio, USA
O'Kelly Isley, singer—born 1937, Cincinatti, Ohio, USA

FROM CINCINATTI, OHIO, THE ISLEY BROTHERS ARE ONE OF THE MOST ACCOMPLISHED GROUPS IN THE HISTORY OF SOUL MUSIC. FROM THE MID-FIFTIES THROUGH TO THIS DAY THEY HAVE SURVIVED THE RIGOURS OF CHANGE BY PERSEVERING, PIONEERING, WRITING AND SINGING SOME OF SOUL MUSIC'S GREATEST CLASSICS.

The three original members were Ronald, Rudolph and O'Kelly who first sang gospel with their mother and a fourth brother who was later killed in a motor accident. In 1957 the three brothers left for New York and recorded for a number of small labels before RCA signed them in 1959. Live in concert the group sang the Jackie Wilson hit 'Lonely Teardrops', at the end of which their ad-libbing got audiences on their feet to stand up and shout. This inspired their first million-seller 'Shout', and later 'Twist And Shout', another million-seller for Atlantic Records in 1962.

In the UK the Beatles scored a huge hit with 'Twist And Shout', but it was Motown Records which made the Isley Brothers international soul stars by teaming them with writers/producers Holland, Dozier and Holland in 1966 for a string of classics, including 'This Old Heart Of Mine' (UK Top 50/US Top 20), 'Take Some Time Out For Love', 'I Guess I'll Always Love You',

'Behind A Painted Smile', and 'Put Yourself In My Place'.

The Isley Brothers were by this time one of the top vocal harmony groups on the soul scene, but times were changing and the group kept one step ahead by embracing a funkier sound set for the Seventies. In 1969 they drifted away from Motown Records, Motown itself soon to ditch its own Detroit sound and head for Los Angeles, the Isleys meanwhile expanding to incorporate two younger brothers—Marvin (bass) and Ernie (drums/guitar)—and a cousin—Chris Jasper (keyboards)—to become a self-contained funk band.

Reviving their own T-Neck label (with which they had originally experimented unsuccessfully in the mid-Sixties) they scored a hit on both sides of the Atlantic with 'It's Your Thing', a song which may have been inspired by James Brown. They also became self-sufficient on material, writing and producing

The Isley Brothers have survived over 30 years of changing times in black music.

original songs which remain standards, often covered by other artists even to this day.

In 1973 the Isley Brothers signed their T-Neck logo to Epic and commenced a third decade in the music business by re-making a song they had cut back in 1964. 'That Lady' from the album *3 + 3* did very little when initially released, but never before had the Jimi Hendrix-inspired guitar work of Ernie Isley been so prominent. Hendrix had in fact been a member of the Isleys' road and studio band during the mid-Sixties, and it was this guitar element that certainly played an important part in keeping the Isleys' sound so vibrant through the Seventies on hits including 'That Lady', 'Highway Of My Life', 'Summer Breeze', 'Harvest For The World', 'Take Me To The Next Phase', 'It's A Disco Night (Rock Don't Stop)' and, in 1983, 'Between The Sheets'.

A parting of ways came in 1984 when the younger members of the group left to form Isley, Jasper And Isley, leaving the original elder brothers to sign to Warner Brothers on their own. However, the older group only managed to record their *Masterpiece* album of 1985 before O'Kelly died of a heart attack in 1986.

In 1987 the group's *Smooth Sailing* album featured only Ronald and Rudolph Isley, but Marvin rejoined the Isley Brothers in 1992 for the release of their most recent album, *Tracks Of Life*.

OTIS REDDING

The Lost Genius of Soul

* * *

Singer/Songwriter
Born: 1941, Dawson, Georgia, USA
Died: 1967, Wisconsin, USA

*O*TIS REDDING HAD ONE OF THE MOST HONEST, HEARTFELT AND EMOTIONAL VOICES IN SOUL MUSIC HISTORY AND THOROUGHLY DESERVES ALL THE RECOGNITION HE HAS ACQUIRED OVER THE YEARS. HE WAS A VISIONARY WHO SANG ABOUT LIFE AND THE HUMAN CONDITION WITH DEEP UNDERSTANDING AND KNOWLEDGE BUT WITHOUT BEING BOMBASTIC OR PREACHING. HIS VOICE WAS GENTLE YET CONFIDENT, IT COULD SING THE ULTIMATE LOVE SONG AND VERY OFTEN DID.

Otis was born in Dawson, Georgia, in 1941, the son of a poor labourer and preacher. He learnt the basics of singing in church, local clubs and listening to the music of his idols such as Sam Cooke. After moving with his family to Macon, Georgia, Otis made two singles for the Confederate label imitating artists Little Richard ('Shout Bamalama') and Barrett Strong ('She's Alright') before hooking up with singer Johnny Jenkins and becoming a member of his backing group the Pinetoppers.

His first single, 'Love Twist', recorded with the group was signed up by Atlantic who subsequently took them to record at Stax's studios in Memphis. Here the Pinetoppers struggled and proved unable to record a follow-up so

the session was cancelled leaving some spare studio time. Otis persuaded the producer and Stax's house band, featuring such distinguished musicians as Al Jackson and Steve Cropper of Booker T's MGs, to record one of his own songs: 'These Arms Of Mine'. Although technically belonging to Atlantic Records, the record was released on Stax's newly-formed Volt subsidiary label in 1962. It only dented the US Top 100, but marked the start of an historic liaison between artist, studio and musicians. By the time Otis signed directly to Atlantic for the release of 'Pain In My Heart' in 1964, he had already been accepted as an exceptional singer and songwriter, and became one of the first singers with that harder edge to his voice which was to become known as "soul". His hits through the mid-Sixties continued with 'That's What My Heart Needs', 'That's How Strong My Love Is', 'I've Been Loving You Too Long', 'Respect', later adapted and recorded by Aretha Franklin, 'My Girl', 'Satisfaction', 'My Lover's Prayer',

'I Can't Turn You Loose', 'Fa Fa Fa Fa (Sad Song)', 'Try A Little Tenderness', 'Day Tripper', 'Let Me Come On Home' and 'Shake'.

He had become one of the most successful soul singers of his time. Credit for this was due also to Otis's manager Phil Walden who had guided his career and, through his success, acquired further clients such as Sam And Dave, Johnnie Taylor, Eddie Floyd and Percy Sledge to become the biggest booking agent for soul artists in the world in the mid-Sixties. All Otis really lacked was true star status which could well have been due to competition from Motown Records in Detroit where their hit factory tended to overshadow everything else happening on the soul scene.

In fact, following the success Marvin Gaye was having with Tammi Terrell, Otis teamed up with Carla Thomas for an album *King And Queen* (1967),

and although hits were scored with 'Tramp' and 'Knock On Wood' from the album, this rootsy R&B combination was commercially not a match for what Motown were able to achieve with their star duo.

The song Otis is no doubt best remembered for is '(Sittin' On) The Dock Of The Bay', his biggest ever hit which remained Number 1 in the US charts for 4 weeks and

reached Number 3 in the UK charts, selling over a million copies. It was released in 1968 but was recorded in 1967, only three days before he was tragically killed.

On December 10, his private plane crashed into Lake Monona in Madison, Wisconsin, killing Otis, his valet, the pilot and four members of his backing group, the Bar-Kays. Redding was only 26 years old when he died.

If Otis had had an opportunity to complete an album off the back of this soul masterpiece he may well have become one of the biggest household names of soul, but 'Dock Of The Bay' was no half-measure and did more than enough to leave a major mark in soul music history.

His final entry into the US charts was with the posthumous single 'Love Man' in 1969, and indeed it is as a man of love that the world perceived him.

Otis Redding, one of the most successful soul singers of all time, is probably best remembered for '(Sittin' On) The Dock Of The Bay'.

WILLIAM "SMOKEY" ROBINSON

The Lyrical Poet of Soul

* * *

Singer/Songwriter/Producer
Born: 1940, Detroit, Michigan, USA

It was his lyrics that were particularly inspiring, Bob Dylan hailing him as the twentieth century's greatest living poet. Vocally, however he was not a typical black

SMOKEY ROBINSON IS AN ARTIST WHO, DURING THE SIXTIES, HELPED TO MAKE MOTOWN THE INTERNATIONAL SUCCESS IT WAS. THROUGH AN ERA WHERE SOUL MUSIC WAS BORN AND BECAME ITS MOST PROLIFIC, SMOKEY WAS WRITING CLASSIC SONGS AND PRODUCING NUMEROUS HITS FOR BOTH HIS OWN GROUP THE MIRACLES AND OTHER PRIORITY MOTOWN ACTS SUCH AS MARVIN GAYE, MARY WELLS AND THE TEMPTATIONS.

In fact he was instrumental in the instigation of soul music itself during his days as a protégé of Motown founder Berry Gordy in the mid Fifties. Gordy had been at the start of soul music's evolution as it derived itself from the R&B-type records he wrote and produced for Jackie Wilson (such as 'Reet Petite'). Further inspired by the success of groups like the Drifters, Berry cultivated Smokey's talent for lyrics, melody and production in a direction that ultimately became known as soul music.

singer; he did not have a soul voice in the traditional sense, it was cool and breezy but not lightweight in its ability to express. It was a voice uniquely his own, managing to convey the content of his songs like no other, and in so doing became popular with both black and white audiences—as did the Motown sound itself, more commonly attributed to writers and producers Holland, Dozier and Holland.

He was born in Detroit, where he wrote his first song when he was 6 years old for a school play in which he also took the lead role. As a teenager, Smokey went to Northern High School where in 1955 he formed the Matadors. Upon meeting Berry Gordy they changed their name to the Miracles and in the days before Motown Berry recorded them and licensed their first singles 'Got A Job' and 'Bad Girl' to End and Chess Records respectively.

'Way Over There' became the first Miracles release via Motown

Smokey Robinson fronted the Miracles but was also one of Motown's most prolific songwriters.

(only the eighth release on their Tamla label), and 'Shop Around' became the group's first US hit. Without any subsequent significant chart success, for about 2 years thereafter came an experimental and learning period in Smokey's career which lead to the group's succession of hits with 'You Really Got A Hold On Me', 'Ooh Baby Baby', 'That's What Love Is Made Of', 'Going To A Go Go', 'I Second That Emotion', 'The Tracks Of My Tears', 'Tears Of A Clown', and 'Baby, Baby Don't Cry'.

The accomplished writing and producing he applied to his own group was now in demand among other Motown artists. He began by writing and producing 'My Guy' for Mary Wells, Motown's first pop hit, but during Motown's heyday he also delivered hits for artists including the Temptations ('The Way You Do The Things You Do', 'My Girl' and 'Get Ready'), Marvin Gaye ('Ain't That Peculiar'), the Marvelettes ('Don't Mess With Bill'), and the Supremes ('Floy Joy' and 'Automatically Sunshine').

In 1971 Smokey left the Miracles to launch a solo career, his position with the group handed to newcomer Billy Griffin who gave the group one last major hit with 'Love Machine' before also departing to commence a solo career (more recently in London where he has co-produced groups like the Pasadenas and Take That with Ian Levine).

Smokey's solo work through the Seventies and Eighties was not so prolific as his time with Motown. After his first album, *Smokey* (1973), hits and the occasional soul classic continued with songs including 'Just My Soul Responding' (1974), 'Cruisin'' (1979, from the album with the same name), 'Being With You' (1981), 'Tell Me Tomorrow' from *Yes It's You Lady* (1982) and 'Just To See Her' (1987).

Being so close to Berry Gordy over the years, it was not surprising that by 1990 Smokey Robinson was vice president at Motown, but when the company was sold to MCA he left as an artist and signed to the SBK label (via EMI) for which he still records today.

DIANA ROSS

The First Lady of Soul

* * *

Singer/Actress
Born: 1944, Detroit, Michigan, USA

*T*HE BLACK FEMALE STAR OF ALL STARS, DIANA ROSS HAS ACHIEVED
WHAT IS UNLIKELY TO BE EVER ACHIEVED AGAIN BY ANY FEMALE ARTIST IN
SOUL MUSIC HISTORY. APPEALING TO ALL, REGARDLESS OF AGE, RACE,
COLOUR AND POSITION, DIANA ROSS IS A LEGEND IN HER OWN TIME,
POSSESSING A VOICE WHICH MANAGES TO REACH OUT AND
TOUCH THE HEART AND SOUL AND SPIRIT OF EVERYONE.

Although subsequent singers may have shown greater technical, more showy
and flamboyant abilities, Diana Ross quite simply sings the song with a deli-
verance so uniquely her own that she cannot be matched on this level.

Furthermore, aside from the honest, straightforward, feminine, sensitive
and ultimately soulful qualities of her voice, Diana Ross is more than a singer,
she's an entity in her own right. Her looks, glitzy persona and reputation as
a hard businesswoman have also played a role in making her the huge success that other, often better, singers have missed out on.

She was born Diane Earle in Detroit, Michigan, in 1944, and in 1960 became
a member of the Supremes, a group formed by Mary Wilson and Florence
Ballard. With the help of mighty music-makers Holland, Dozier and Holland,
and mighty image-makers Motown Records, the Supremes became the most
successful girl group of all time,
Diana's superior vocal skills and solo
ambitions pushing her centre stage.
In 1967 the group became known
as Diana Ross And The Supremes
while Motown orchestrated her
departure from the group to commence her inevitable solo career,
which was launched in 1969.

With the departure of Holland,
Dozier and Holland from Motown,
and the company's relocation to Los
Angeles, Diana began a collaboration
with writers/producers Nick Ashford
and Valerie Simpson who engineered her initial solo hits 'Reach
Out And Touch (Somebody's
Hand)', 'Ain't No Mountain High
Enough' (UK Top 10, US Number
1), and 'Remember Me' (UK Top
10), which helped turn her into a
soul superstar in the early Seventies.

For the next 10 years Diana
remained at Motown, broadening
her horizons into film (as Billie
Holiday in *Lady Sings The Blues*,
fashion designer Tracey Chambers in
Mahogany and Dorothy in *The Wiz*)
and dominating the charts with a
string of hits including 'Remember

Me', 'I'm Still Waiting' (UK Number 1), 'Surrender' (UK Top 10), 'Doobedood'ndoobe Doobedood'ndoobe', 'Touch Me In The Morning' (UK Top 10/US Number 1), 'All Of My Life' (UK Top 10), 'You Are Everything' with Marvin Gaye (UK Top 5, 'Last Time I Saw Him' (UK Top 40), 'Stop Look Listen (To Your Heart)' with Marvin Gaye (UK Top 25), 'Love Me' (UK Top 40), 'Sorry Doesn't Always Make It Right' (UK Top 25), 'Theme From Mahogany' (UK Top 5/US Number 1), 'Love Hangover' (UK Top 10/US Number 1), 'I Thought It Took A Little Time' (UK Top 40), 'Gettin' Ready For Love' (UK Top 25), 'Lovin', Livin' And Givin'' (UK Top 75), 'The Boss' (UK Top 40), 'No One Gets The Prize' (UK Top 60), 'It's My House' (UK Top 40), 'Upside Down' (UK Top 5/US Number 1), 'My Old Piano' (UK Top 5), 'I'm Coming Out' (UK Top 20/US Top 5), 'It's My Turn' (UK Top 20/US Top 10), 'One More Chance' (UK Top 50), and, in 1981, 'Cryin' My Heart Out For You' (UK Top 60).

Diana Ross, the Supreme who became the Boss.

She left Motown in 1981 after 'Endless Love' (UK Top 10/US Number 1), a duet with Lionel Richie, before signing to Capitol/EMI (RCA in the US) for the period of her career which took her away from soul into a more pop idiom with songs including 'Why Do Fools Fall In Love' (UK Top 5/US Top 10). She also charted at Capitol with 'It's Never Too Late', 'Muscles' (UK Top 20/US Top 10), 'So Close', 'Pieces Of Ice', 'Touch By Touch', 'Eaten Alive', 'Chain Reaction' (UK Number 1), 'Experience', 'Dirty Looks' and 'Mr. Lee'.

In the UK, Diana's recordings continue to be released via EMI, while her American releases have reverted back to Motown. Diana owns several companies, including her own label, Ross Records.

THE TEMPTATIONS

The Quintessential Soul Quintet

* * *

Eddie Kendricks — born 1939, Union Springs, Alabama, USA
Paul Williams — born 1939, Birmingham, Alabama, USA
Melvin Franklin — born 1942, Montgomery, Alabama, USA
Otis Williams — born 1941, Texarkana, Texas, USA
David Ruffin — born 1941, Meridian, Mississippi, USA

*M*UCH LIKE THE FOUR TOPS, THE TEMPTATIONS ARE ONE OF THE FEW SUPER GROUPS OF THE SIXTIES TO SURVIVE THROUGH TO THE NINETIES. SIMILARLY THEY WERE BORN AND BRED AT MOTOWN LIKE SO MANY SOUL STARS (MARVIN GAYE, DIANA ROSS, STEVIE WONDER, SMOKEY ROBINSON, MICHAEL JACKSON, ETC.), ALTHOUGH UNLIKE THE FOUR TOPS THEY HAVE UNDERGONE NUMEROUS PERSONNEL CHANGES OVER THE YEARS.

A vocal group, Paul Williams, Otis Williams, Melvin Franklin, Eddie Kendricks and Elbridge Bryant were scattered among local Detroit groups the Primes, the Elgins, the Pirates, the Distants and the Voicemasters before coming together as the Temptations in 1960. Signing to Motown Records, they teamed up with Smokey Robinson who had been a high school friend and a protégé of Motown boss Berry Gordy. Their first collaboration, 'I Want A Love I Can See' (1963), won encouraging local support.

In 1964 the departure of Elbridge Bryant left a vacancy for lead singer soon filled by David Ruffin, and although it was Eddie Kendricks who fronted 'The Way You Do The Things You Do', the first successful collaboration between the group and writer/producer Smokey Robinson, all ears were on David Ruffin who was one of the most exciting new soul voices of the Sixties.

The Temptations had originally offered the lead position to brother Jimmy Ruffin, but wanting to concentrate on a solo career he handed it to David, an intensely soulful vocalist who, with Smokey Robinson's songs and productions, took the group to international stardom with songs including 'My Girl', 'Since I Lost My Baby', 'Don't Look Back', and 'It's Growing'.

With the Supremes becoming known as Diana Ross And The Supremes, David wanted the Temptations renamed David Ruffin And The Temptations, a proposition rejected by Motown, which ultimately led to his departure from the group to commence a solo career. It was Dennis Edwards who then stepped in as this replacement in 1969 for more hits, most notably 'I Can't Get Next To You', 'Cloud Nine', and their collaboration with Diana Ross And The Supremes on albums *T.C.B.*, *Together* and a TV special *Taking Care Of Business*.

With the demise of the Motown sound, caused partly by the less than amicable departure of Holland, Dozier and Holland, partly by the company's relocation to Los Angeles, and partly by inevitable change itself, the Temptations made a milestone record with 'Papa Was A Rolling Stone' (US Number 1 in 1972). It was produced by Norman Whitfield who had already given the group such hits as 'Beauty Is Only Skin Deep', 'Ain't Too Proud To Beg', 'I Wish It Would Rain', 'I Can't Get Next To You' (US Number 1) and 'Just My Imagination'

(US Number 1), not to mention being the creator of Marvin Gaye's 'I Heard It Through the Grapevine'.

With 'Papa Was A Rolling Stone' (and his work with Undisputed Truth), Norman helped pioneer a funkier form of black music for the Seventies which utilized a fuse of strings, synthesizers and wah-wah guitar with new rhythm ideas which, in straight R&B, was to inspire Curtis Mayfield and, in R&B pop circles, the likes of Barry White.

The group had undergone other personnel changes by this time too. Paul Williams left for health reasons and was replaced by Richard Street, and in 1971 Dennis Edwards handed the lead over to Eddie

Kendricks for one of the group's finest moments: 'Just My Imagination'. Further changes were to follow when Eddie left to be replaced by Damon Harris for the *All Directions* album (1973). He in turn was replaced by Glenn Leonard.

The Temptations continued to record successfully at Motown through to 1977 when they moved briefly to Atlantic Records for albums *Here To Tempt You* (1977) and *Bare Back* (1978) by which time Louis Price was lead singer and Ron Tyson was a new addition to the group. Since 1980 they have been back with Motown where through different producers and further personnel adjustments (most notably Ollie Woodson becoming lead singer), they have both recorded and toured consistently with occasional hit success such as 'Standing On the Top' from the 1982 *Reunion* album which featured both David Ruffin and Eddie Kendricks, 'Treat Her Like A Lady' and 'Look What You Started'.

One of the many line-ups in the Temptations in over 20 years in the business.

STEVIE WONDER

The Masterblaster of Soul

* * *

Singer/Keyboards/Songwriter/Producer
Born: 1950, Saginaw, Michigan, USA

*S*TEVIE WONDER IS MORE THAN A SOUL LEGEND, HE IS AN OUTSTANDING MUSICAL PHENOMENON. ASIDE FROM BEING VIRTUALLY THE GREATEST BLIND MUSICIAN OF THE TWENTIETH CENTURY (WITH THE NOTABLE EXCEPTION OF RAY CHARLES), STEVIE EMERGED FROM HIS DAYS AS THE FRAGILE-LOOKING KID WITH A BIG VOICE TO BE A MUSICAL INNOVATOR AND SOCIALLY CONSCIOUS LYRICIST (COMMITTED TO SOCIAL HARMONY) LOADED WITH TALENT, ENERGY AND ENTHUSIASM.

Only Michael Jackson and Prince come close to the genius of Stevie Wonder, although in classic soul terms he is unchallenged for his naturalness of song and voice. He has an extraordinary sense of melody, imaginative vocals and immense creative expression. He has been a major influence on many artists of his time and since and has inspired every artist to some degree.

Alongside the outstanding songs he penned for himself, there are many who have benefited from his tremendous songwriting skills, while through his tireless campaigning and sponsored marches in Washington he successfully got Dr Martin Luther King's birthday (January 15) turned into an American national holiday.

He was born Steveland Morris in Saginaw, Michigan, in 1950 and moved to Detroit in the late Fifties where his uncle gave him his first harmonica. It was Ronnie White (of the Miracles) who first recognized the young Stevie's potential and took him to Motown Records where he auditioned for Brian Holland, a Motown executive and a third of the legendary Holland, Dozier and Holland partnership.

Motown signed him in 1960 and changed his name to Little Stevie Wonder. He made his début with 'I Call It Pretty Music (But The Old People Call It The Blues)', but it was 'Fingertips' in 1963 that firmly established him and enabled him to tour with the Motor Town Revue during the mid-Sixties. While 'Fingertips' topped the American singles chart, its parent album *The Twelve Year Old Genius* simultaneously topped the US albums chart—the first time this ever happened in the US Billboard system. (He was still so young at the time that Motown became his legal guardian and took care of his education with private tutors).

There was concern at Motown however in 1965 when Stevie's voice broke, but amid rumours he would be dropped by the label he teamed up with staff songwriter Sylvia Moy and wrote 'Uptight', proving his ability as a songwriter too. The record saved his career.

By 1970 Stevie's novelty value as a child star had been superseded by his much more mature approach to his music. Hit songs such as 'Blowin' In The Wind', 'A Place In The Sun', 'I Was Made To Love Her', 'I'm Wondering', 'For Once In My Life', 'I Don't Know Why' and 'My Cherie Amour' had given audiences a new perspective. In 1970 he married Syreeta Wright.

On his twenty-first birthday, Stevie took up an option to be released by Motown. The company was no longer legally responsible for him, and money that was held by Motown on his behalf was paid across to him. Furthermore a rift had developed as Motown wanted Stevie to stick to their proven hit-making formulas, but while recognizing that commercialism was important to record sales, Stevie felt he could still be successful by developing his own creativity and being original. He therefore took two years off to build his own recording studio and experiment with new sounds.

When he returned to Motown in 1972 he delivered an album, *Music Of My Mind*, on which he played virtually every instrument, and by the release of his *Talking Book* album—which included 'Superstition' and 'You Are The Sunshine Of My Life'—he had helped push black music into the era of synthesizer/keyboards-dominated music aided by advanced recording techniques.

In 1973 he released probably his most highly acclaimed and Grammy award-winning album, *Innervisions*—which included 'Higher Ground' and 'Living For The City' —before a near-fatal car crash left him in a

Stevie Wonder, a true musical genius.

coma for 4 days. Fully recovering within 8 weeks he continued to build his now legendary status with such hits as 'He's Misstra Know It All', 'Boogie On Reggae Woman', 'You Haven't Done Nothin', 'Don't You Worry 'Bout A Thing', 'I Wish', 'Sir Duke', 'Another Star', 'Send One Your Love', 'Masterblaster', 'I Ain't Gonna Stand For It', 'Lately', 'That Girl' and 'Do I Do', 'I Just Called To Say I Love You' and 'Part Time Lover'. His recent works are not as great, but he remains the most important black male singer/songwriter/producer in all soul music.

soul classics

ANITA BAKER

RAPTURE
ELEKTRA, 1986

THE ADVANCEMENT IN ELEC-TRONIC TECHNOLOGY IN THE EIGHTIES LED TO A MOVE AWAY FROM THE RAW, UNRESTRAINED gospel stylings of the Sixties and Seventies and a trend towards more sophisticated jazz-tinged vocal techniques as displayed superbly on this, Anita's second album.

Upon release, *Rapture* not only catapulted Anita Baker to international acclaim, but has also since become recognized by many as *the* classic female soul album of the entire decade. (Her *Songstress* début was as highly acclaimed critically, but lacked the same commercial success).

Produced almost entirely by Michael J. Powell, this consistent release represents a fine showcase of Anita's disciplined, yet deeply impassioned, bittersweet vocal expertise on a set of eight mellow love songs complemented perfectly by some subtle musical arrangements.

The album's best-known track is undoubtedly the hit 'Sweet Love', with its familiar, thumping piano riffs and sophisticated strings, though the real gem is the hauntingly melodic 'Caught Up In The Rapture'. Elsewhere, the jazz influence is felt most strongly on the slinkily weaving 'Been So Long' (complete with some impressive scatting). The tuneful 'Same Ole Love' was a US hit single in 1987.

In addition to Anita's own compositions, such as the crisp, rousing 'Watch Your Step', the album boasts some impressive contributions from noted songwriters like Rod Temperton ('Mystery') and David Lasley ('You Bring Me Joy'). Meanwhile the punchy shuffler 'Number 1 In The World' injects a different brassy flavour.

Throughout Anita's low register, subtly impassioned vocals soar and glide distinctively alongside some of the West Coast's finest session musicians to create a timeless masterpiece of jazz-tinged, sophisticated soul.

BOOKER T AND THE MGs

BEST OF BOOKER T AND THE MGs
STAX, 1971

*C*ALYPSO FANS MIGHT BE DIS-
APPOINTED THAT 'TIME IS
TIGHT' IS NOT INCLUDED HERE.
NOR, FOR THAT MATTER IS ANY-
thing which the Stax number one
session band cut following the company's sale to Gulf & Western/
Paramount in 1969. But these are
the best of the classic cuts recorded during the near-legendary
Stax/Atlantic era, when the
Memphis company's product was
distributed by the bigger New York-
based set-up, and the Ertegun brothers and Jerry Wexler—the triumvirate which headed Atlantic's
operations—had a very real input
into what went down.

The album kicks off with the
moody 'Green Onions', the potent

début number which thrust Booker
T And The MGs onto the international scene back in 1962, earning
a gold disc in the process.

Booker T. Jones on keyboards,
Steve Cropper on lead guitar and Al
Jackson Jr. on drums were joined by
Lewis Steinberg on bass. Immediately after the hit, Steinberg was
replaced by Donald "Duck" Dunn,
who came from the Mar-Keys, with
which outfit Steve Cropper had also
served his apprenticeship.

To a degree the Mar-Keys and
the MGs were almost one group.
They acted as horn section and
rhythm section respectively and
played on each other's records as
well as many of the other great hits
to emanate from the Stax studios,
not only for such Stax acts as Rufus
and Carla Thomas, Sam And Dave,
William Bell and Eddie Floyd but for
Atlantic artists including Don Covay
and Wilson Pickett.

Booker T And The MGs effectively defined the funky southern
gutbucket sound which became
known as "the Memphis beat"—
instrumental soul at its best.

BOYZ II MEN

COOLEYHIGHHARMONY
MOTOWN, 1991

*W*ITH AMERICAN SALES EXCEED-
ING 4 MILLION, THIS AUSPI-
CIOUS DÉBUT BY THE YOUNG
PHILADELPHIA QUARTET IS NOW OFFI-
cially the best-selling album by a
male soul vocal group in US history. Boyz II Men have also become
the group who have brought
Motown's legacy of outstanding
vocal groups through to the Nineties
with a vengeance, while simultaneously breaking the new generation
of urban funk (new jack swing) on
the mainstream pop scene.

The LP is divided neatly between
ballad and dance material, the former made up of dreamy, romantic
shufflers typified by the US hit
'Uhh Ahh', while the foursome's
impeccable harmonies shone best on
their refreshing a cappella rendition
of 'It's So Hard To Say Goodbye
To Yesterday'. The up tempos

meanwhile were mostly of the new jack swing variety and introduced the anthemic 'Motownphilly'—a stunning combination of faultless old-school soul harmonies with the tough street beats of the Nineties. The album eventually topped the UK charts on its highly publicized re-release in October 1992, by which time the Boyz' US Number 1 ballad 'End Of The Road' (taken from the *Boomerang* movie soundtrack) had been added to the initial track listing, along with remixes of several of the album's original cuts—including the heavy underground club favourite 'Sympi'.

JAMES BROWN

LIVE AT THE APOLLO
POLYGRAM, 1962

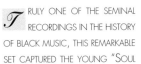 RULY ONE OF THE SEMINAL RECORDINGS IN THE HISTORY OF BLACK MUSIC, THIS REMARKABLE SET CAPTURED THE YOUNG "SOUL

Brother Number 1" at his wildest, tearing up the audience at soul music's greatest shrine—the Apollo Theatre in New York's Harlem. Cut before the days of the equally epoch-making 'Get Up I Feel Like Being A Sex Machine' and 'Cold Sweat', which kicked the whole funk thing into top gear, and even before the mod anthems 'Papa's Got A Brand New Bag' and 'I Feel Good', this atmosphere-laden performance captures the boss, already dubbed "the hardest-working man in show-business", long before his dazzling on-stage moves and totally uninhibited vocal histrionics had become parodies of themselves.

This is raw, fresh, vital talent, recorded six years after he first hit the charts with 'Please Please Please' but in advance of his greatest triumphs. 'Try Me' is the man at his very finest, wringing every ounce of emotion out of a potent gospel-style ballad, while the instrumental 'Night Train' reveals that, even in those far-off days, James was already surrounding himself with the very finest musicians.

It was the kind of high-energy, no-holds-barred show which he was to present to British audiences when he made his UK début several years later, by which time his backing singers and dancers, the Famous Flames and the JBs, had been honed into the most exciting package show in the business.

THE DRIFTERS

BEST OF THE DRIFTERS
PICKWICK/ATLANTIC, 1986

TILL GOING STRONG TODAY, 40 YEARS AFTER BEING FORMED IN NEW YORK, THE DRIFTERS ARE LIKE A GREAT FOOTBALL team—singers may come and go (and there have been more than 50 so far) but the group rolls on for ever, now under the guidance of manager Faye Treadwell. The outfit, which in many ways defined the uptown soul group idiom, now has none of its original members left, though Johnnie Moore did join very early on and still fronts the current line-up after spells out for military service.

This superbly representative selection of the Drifters at their very best comes from the Atlantic Records group's golden era in the early Sixties when the hits seemed to be truly non-stop, thanks not only to the great vocals and superb production but to wonderfully evocative songs, many of them from the pens of Leiber and Stoller, who were also busy churning out hits for the Coasters, Elvis Presley and others. There are cuts featuring Ben E. King as lead singer, others with the late Rudy Lewis's peerless voice at the helm, and yet others with Johnnie Moore in command.

'There Goes My Baby', 'On Broadway', 'Save The Last Dance For Me', 'Saturday Night At The Movies', 'Under The Boardwalk'— here's a whole slew of songs which transcend the soul idiom, capturing the mood of just what it was like being a teenager in the Sixties.

ARETHA FRANKLIN

BEST OF ARETHA FRANKLIN
ATLANTIC, 1986

*T*HE DAUGHTERS OF A PREACHER, ARETHA FRANKLIN AND HER SISTERS ERMA AND CAROLYN— BOTH OF WHOM ALSO FOUND recording success—were schooled in gospel music from an early age, receiving encouragement from such formidable talents as Sam Cooke, Dinah Washington and Whitney Houston's mother Cissy, who was a close relative. Their father, the Rev. C. L. Franklin, issued more than 80 albums of hot sermonizing during a long career and there was also a strong jazz influence in Aretha's early upbringing, her initial recordings being a mix of the gospel and jazz styles.

That background and an enormous innate talent enabled Aretha to develop into an artist who truly merits her tag "Queen of Soul".

While such stars as Diana Ross, Etta James, Esther Phillips, Gladys Knight and Nina Simone have all made their own contributions to soul music history, it is Aretha who stands out clearly as the greatest of them all.

It helped, of course, that—once signed to Atlantic—she had the support of great musicians, including such worthies as guitarists Joe South and Eric Gale, bass player Jerry Jemmott and sax maestro King Curtis, plus the formidable Sweet Inspirations vocal back-up team (lead by Cissy Houston) who also worked with Elvis Presley.

Wizard producer Jerry Wexler and arranger Arif Mardin also made a major contribution, so too did an inspired choice of material. But whether on originals like 'Chain Of Fools' (especially penned for her by Don Covay), the spine-tingling ballad 'You Make Me Feel Like A Natural Woman' and the blues-tinged 'Doctor Feelgood', or on cover versions of Otis Redding's 'Respect' and Ben E. King's 'Spanish Harlem', Aretha's own unique creativity always shone through.

121

MARVIN GAYE

WHAT'S GOING ON
MOTOWN, 1971

*R*EGARDED BY MANY AS THE ULTIMATE CLASSIC SOUL ALBUM, THIS LANDMARK RELEASE MARKED MARVIN GAYE'S PRO-gression from the distinctive Sixties Motown vocalist to a credible, respected singer/songwriter/producer whose socially conscious lyrics echoed the awareness and unrest of the new soul generation of the early Seventies.

The turn of the decade had seen US civil rights marches combining with anti-Vietnam protests to create a turbulent social climate in America. This was accurately reflected in Marvin's touching pleas for tolerance and peace on classic cuts like the haunting title song and the sombre 'What's Happening Brother'.

Meanwhile his heartfelt environmental warning on the lilting 'Mercy Mercy Me (The Ecology)', complete

with his sensitive anti-drug stance on the confused and complex 'Flying High (In The Friendly Sky)' are timeless messages that ring as true today as they did 20 years ago.

Emotionally, on the other hand, the spiritual intensity of the slow ballads 'God Is Love' and 'Wholly Holy' is matched only by the phenomenal emotion conveyed in Marvin's mournful delivery of the moving anthem 'Save The Children'.

From a musical angle, this album also made a radical break from the previous on-the-fours stomping Motown sound of the Sixties, and instead lay the matrix for the Seventies with its conga-driven, mid-tempo rhythms enhanced by haunting strings, lazily drifting sax and ethereal multi-layered vocal harmonies. All of this gelled to create an unusual lilting jazz flavour.

Meanwhile, a funkier flavour was introduced on the subtly hypnotic 'Inner City Blues (Make Me Wanna Holler)', a powerful bass line underlying a solidly building groove to depict the bleak stark realities of ghetto life. This is a timeless masterpiece that displayed amazing lyrical insight into the world's problems, while providing the first glimpse of the sadly troubled inner mind of a highly sensitive and tragic genius.

ISAAC HAYES

HOT BUTTERED SOUL
STAX, 1969

WHEN THE MASSIVE GULF & WESTERN CONGLOMERATE'S PARAMOUNT SUBSIDIARY BURST ON TO THE RECORD SCENE WITH AN open cheque book in 1969, Stax Records' founders Jim Stewart and Estelle Axton (Stax being the first two letters of their respective surnames) were quick to succumb, selling their company in a headline-grabbing mega-deal.

Anxious to make an immediate impact on the black music scene, the new owners decided on a massive new release schedule which found Stax artists and session musician teams working on a shift system to churn out a 27-album binge in the space of just two weeks.

Standing head and shoulders above everything else was *Hot Buttered Soul*, a truly remarkable album and only Hayes's second as an artist as opposed to producer or songwriter—the first *Presenting Isaac Hayes* (later retitled *Blue Hayes*), back in 1967, having been the result of a late-night jam session when someone left the studio tape running.

Featuring just four tracks, *Hot Buttered Soul* was truly a watershed in soul music, ushering in the concept album, the symphonic soul idiom, the extended song and the spoken rap all at the same time. Isaac's remake of Dionne Warwick's 'Walk On By' remains a masterpiece, building the mood layer by layer much after the fashion of Ravel's *Bolero*.

MICHAEL JACKSON

THRILLER
EPIC, 1982

WITH GLOBAL SALES IN EXCESS OF 40 MILLION, *THRILLER* IS NOW FAR AND AWAY THE BIGGEST-SELLING ALBUM OF ALL TIME IN ANY musical category. To black music lovers, the stomping 'Billie Jean' represents Michael at his absolute peak, with its powerfully pulsating bass line, stunning string arrangement and realistic storyline. Meanwhile, for the pop scene, the "horror spoof" title track is his most memorable recording, its magnetically infectious chorus and relentless rhythm track pounding alongside the famous eerie sound-effects and brilliantly ghoulish Vincent Price "rap", all later portrayed so memorably in the epic and ground-breaking *Thriller* video—a mini-movie with extra dialogue and elements not on the record itself.

Musically, mid-tempo-paced highlights include the finger-snapping Paul McCartney duet 'The Girl Is Mine', its appealing melody offset by shuffling rhythms and subtle orchestration, while the gently undulating 'Human Nature' sees Jackson's breathy vocals perfectly enhancing the song's haunting atmospheric qualities. The danceable side of Jackson meanwhile is strongly represented by the forceful chants and compelling percussion of the rhythmic 'Wanna Be Startin' Somethin'', and the crisp bounce of 'P.Y.T. (Pretty Young Thing)'. Elsewhere the irrepressible 'Beat It' (with howling Eddie Van Halen guitar solo) represents one of the few successful "soul meets rock" ventures of the early Eighties.

In retrospect, the greatest achievement of *Thriller* was probably to demonstrate how its inventive and brilliant mixture of different popular music cultures and styles of the time could realistically transform a black teen idol into one of the most universally accepted and charismatic stars ever.

CURTIS MAYFIELD

SUPERFLY
CURTOM, 1973

UBBED "THE GENTLE GENIUS OF SOUL" FOR HIS MILD, UNASSUMING MANNER AND DISTINCTIVE HIGH TENOR VOICE, CURTIS Mayfield has nevertheless had a tremendous impact on the development of black American pride and consciousness.

Released on his own Curtom label, the multi-million-selling soundtrack *Superfly* was Curtis's fourth solo album, and is virtually his best-remembered work. Echoing its movie's theme of a violent war between two Harlem drug gangs, the album was hailed as a true barometer of the times with its realistic depiction of the drug scene and its accompanying ills.

Musically, the sophisticated orchestration sweeps across the solid conga-driven rhythm tracks creating a dark, moody atmosphere to emphasize the bleak, lyrical warning of songs like the chilling 'Little Child Running Wild' and the relentless 'Pusherman'. Meanwhile the more elaborate piano and strings of lighter rhythm cuts like the haunting 'Give Me Your Love' and irresistible 'No Thing On Me' typify the gliding, breezy Chicago soul sound of the day and can in retrospect be seen as the true roots of that city's modern-day house music scene.

Elsewhere, Curtis's gentle, bittersweet falsetto is stunningly heartfelt and sensitive on the pretty, mid-tempo 'Eddie You Should Know Better', while the fast and furious 'Junkie Chase' and the lazily loping 'Think' highlight Mayfield's fantastic guitar prowess.

THE O'JAYS

COLLECTORS' ITEMS
PHILADELPHIA INTERNATIONAL, 1977

HOUGH ACTUALLY FROM CLEVELAND, OHIO, THE SMOOTH-HARMONIZING O'JAYS WERE TYPICAL OF THE CLASSIC Philadelphia sound which swept the disco world during the dance-crazy Seventies. As the cuts on this highly listenable "best of" selection readily testify, their work shows a wide variety—from the insistent, pulsating neo-funk of 'Back Stabbers' to the smooth uptown soul silkiness of ballads like 'Darling Darling Baby'.

The O'Jays' stylish output for Philadelphia International always bore the distinctive stamp of label bosses and ace producers Kenny Gamble and Leon Huff, enveloping the quartet in the rich musical framework of the potent MFSB studio band with the string sound provided courtesy of the Philadelphia Symphony Orchestra.

Along with label mates Harold Melvin And The Blue Notes and the Intruders, the classy O'Jays gave the Motown hordes a run for their money at a time when the sophisticated soul scene was at its most competitive. As lead singer, Eddie Levert was a worthy challenger to such other soul group heroes as the Four Tops' Levi Stubbs, the Chi-Lites' Eugene Record and the Blue Notes' Teddy Pendergrass.

ALEXANDER O'NEAL

HEARSAY
TABU, 1987

THE EIGHTIES SAW THE UNLIKELY SETTING OF MINNEAPOLIS, MINNESOTA (PREVIOUSLY THE EPITOME OF THE WHITE AMERICAN Midwest) emerge as a prominent black music capital, with local boys Jimmy Jam and Terry Lewis becoming one of the most prolific songwriting/production teams of the decade. This release marked their second album collaboration with

long-time friend and singing discovery Alexander O'Neal.

The trademark Jam and Lewis combination of a funky bass 'n' beats bottom with richly layered melodic synthesized keyboards on top is instantly recognizable on mid-tempo soul rollers like the pounding title track and the solid track 'The Lovers', the latter also boasting some brilliantly creative string lines.

In terms of up-tempo dance-floor cuts, Jam and Lewis demonstrate their versatility as they move from the aggressive, declamatory funk of the chart-toppers 'Criticize', '(What Can I Say) To Make You Love Me' and 'Fake' to the surging, lushly melodic 'Never Knew Love Like This', which sees Alex's powerful tenor duetting with the shrill gospel-like tones of female vocalist and regular duetting companion Cherelle. Meanwhile, both Alex and his producers stress their ballad prowess, as the tender 'Sunshine' leads into the reflective 'Crying Overtime', eventually ending with the sensual, hypnotic closing track 'When The Party's Over'.

Throughout, Alexander's distinctive, slightly cracked tenor ranges from tender masculine vulnerability to growling macho aggression, a recognizable vocal characteristic which sets him apart from smoother male soul balladeers.

WILSON PICKETT

BEST OF WILSON PICKETT
ATLANTIC, RE-RELEASED 1991

*W*ILSON PICKETT'S IMPASSIONED LEAD VOCAL ON THE FALCONS' STUNNING 'I FOUND A LOVE', RECORDED FOR DETROIT LABEL Lupine in 1961, stands as one of the greatest soul ballad performances of all time. It was an outing which, with its mix of gospel fervour and secular blues themes, very much defined the whole idiom.

But the song for which "the wicked Pickett" will always be best remembered is the up-tempo 'Midnight Hour', an item which was so widely covered by aspiring British and European R&B bands in its era that it became something of a sock-it-to-me cliché.

While he was signed to Atlantic up in New York, Wilson's early solo hits belong very much to the renowned Memphis sound. Later, he was to cut equally potent records in both Muscle Shoals and Philadelphia, but it was the Memphis outings, recorded in 1964 and 1965, which brought the man his greatest commercial success.

In 'Mustang Sally', 'Ninety Nine And A Half Won't Do', 'Don't Fight It', 'I'm A Midnight Mover', 'Land Of A Thousand Dances', 'Soul Dance Number Three'—Wilson Pickett's mastery made him a charter member of Atlantic's formidable soul. A quick-tempered and at times viciously unpredictable man who fully earned his "wicked Pickett" epithet—he once chased the Isley brothers through a hotel, firing off a revolver, after losing at cards—Wilson was one of the truly great voices of soul music.

OTIS REDDING

OTIS BLUE
ATCO, 1965

*O*NLY AVAILABLE AT THE TIME ON IMPORT, A COPY OF OTIS REDDING'S WONDERFUL *OTIS BLUE* ALBUM, CONSPICUOUSLY TUCKED under the arm, was an essential part of the uniform for any self-respecting mod during the heady summer of 1965—along with the mohair suit, tab-collar shirt and Cuban-heeled boots.

Otis had first impinged on general consciousness with his début single 'These Arms Of Mine', cut on the tail-end of a Johnny Jenkins And The Pinetoppers' session at the legendary Stax studios in 1962. The subsequent *Pain In My Heart* and *The Great Otis Redding Sings Soul Ballads* albums confirmed our main man as a master of the impassioned slowie, but by the time of *Otis Blue* he was ready to broaden his horizons and this was to be the most satisfying and rounded of all his albums.

For starters, there was a cover of the Temptations' magical 'My Girl' which was every bit as good as the original and which, while not straying far from its inspiration, managed to avoid plagiarism. Then Otis breathed fresh life into 'Shake', a number first recorded by his greatest influence, the late Sam Cooke. A frenetic reading of 'Satisfaction' turned the Rolling Stones' ditty right on its head and 'Down In The Valley' was every bit as good as the Solomon Burke version which had first turned Otis onto the traditional song in the first place.

Then there was a mighty version of B. B. King's 'Rock Me Baby'

which showed that, given a different set of circumstances, Otis could have become a great blues singer.

Nor was it cover versions all the way for, returning to the deep soul ballads, Otis offered up the stunning 'I've Been Loving You Too Long', a truly original masterpiece (co-penned by Otis himself with Jerry Butler) which single-handedly defined just what soul music is all about.

LIONEL RICHIE

CAN'T SLOW DOWN
MOTOWN, 1983

*I*N 1982 LIONEL RICHIE LEFT THE SUCCESSFUL, SELF-CON-TAINED BALLAD/FUNK OUTFIT THE COMMODORES TO PURSUE A MULTI-million-dollar solo career, which saw him become far and away the most successful black singer/songwriter of the Eighties. This second solo album became one of Motown's

biggest-selling albums ever and spawned five major pop hits.

The biggest of these was the spring 1984 chart-topper 'Hello', an ageless slice of evocative, romantic balladry, its lonely, wistful atmosphere enhanced by a haunting melody and sensitive guitar solo. Meanwhile, in a similarly pop-slanted ballad vein were the two follow-up singles: the irresistibly tuneful 'Penny Lover', and the lilting country-styled 'Stuck On You', both of which achieved hit status.

The danceable side of Richie's talent, on the other hand, was most prominently represented by the Caribbean-tinged, anthemic 'All Night Long (All Night)'. Its good-time chants, tribal percussion and infectious climaxes created an explosively joyous, spiritual groove which peaked in autumn 1983 at Number 2 in the UK listings.

Meanwhile, stressing his versatility, Lionel injected a soft rock flavour into the album's other up-tempo hit, the chirpy, uplifting 'Running With The Night', the pounding rhythm of which was

matched by some biting guitar work. Of the remaining tracks, the moody, mid-tempo rippler 'Love Will Find A Way' found greatest favour with the soul crowd, while the bass-prodded jiggler 'Can't Slow Down' recalled Richie's funk days of the Seventies (though was disappointingly weak on melody). Finally, the tender, slushy 'The Only One' possessed a pretty singalong chorus, though remains the album's least-known cut.

Overall, this album is a timeless set of strong commercial songs, whose universal mainstream appeal finally established Lionel Richie with a worldwide crossover audience.

THE STYLISTICS

THE BEST OF THE STYLISTICS
AVCO/AMHERST, 1975

*B*EFORE THE ADVENT OF MICHAEL JACKSON'S *THRILLER*, THE STYLISTICS' DÉBUT ALBUM FOR AVCO WAS JUST ABOUT THE biggest-selling set in the history of black music—virtually every track being a US hit single. That landmark LP is not available on CD but this collection includes its biggest gems and much more besides from Philadelphia's first supergroup.

In the half-decade between 1971 and 1975, the Stylistics couldn't seem to put a foot wrong, their ultra-smooth harmonies framing the seductively sweet and pure high tenor lead vocals of Russell Thompkins Jr. They had taken off when, following earlier success as producer for the Delfonics, the multi-talented Thom Bell assumed a similar role for these newcomers.

Besides his prowess behind the mixing desk, Bell, with his partner Linda Creed, contributed songs which were perfect for the moment.

This was sophisticated uptown soul at its finest, with cuts like 'You Are Everything', 'Betcha By Golly Wow' and 'I'm Stone In Love With You' becoming smooch-time favourites at discos around the world. And, with the quirky 'Rock 'n' Roll Baby', the fivesome showed they could produce appealing up-tempo items too.

When Thom Bell decided to concentrate his efforts behind the Detroit Spinners, the Stylistics found a new production genius in Van McCoy who brought them a second run of hits.

A switch to the then super-hot Philadelphia International label did not work for them, despite the return of Thom Bell as their principal songwriter. Nearly two decades later, the group is still working prodigiously off the back of those stupendous early hits for, while they've barely recorded recently, they remain a major concert draw.

THE TEMPTATIONS

MASTERPIECE
MOTOWN, 1973

*T*HE TEMPTATIONS WILL ALWAYS BE REMEMBERED AS PIONEERS OF THE MOTOWN SOUND IN THE SIXTIES, YET IN TERMS OF MAIN-stream acceptance, their most successful period undoubtedly occurred during the early Seventies when they worked with Motown's charismatic writer/producer genius Norman Whitfield. Taken from that period, this landmark release to many represents the epitome of one of the most successful artist/producer liaisons in black music.

While some critics have occasionally dismissed Whitfield's epic productions as "samey", the two tracks that originally comprised the entire first side of this classic album are, on the contrary, a fine testimony to his versatility. Here, the dreamy, intimate ballad 'Hey Girl' with its sweet harmonies leads into the famous 13-minute plus marathon title cut—a bleak atmospheric depiction of early Seventies black ghetto life in America. Arranger Paul Riser's elaborate orchestration sits atop a relentless bass riff and tapping percussion to create in *Masterpiece* one of Whitfield's most celebrated and chillingly dramatic recordings ever; and while his sparing (if effective) use of the Temptations' vocals have evoked criticisms of Whitfield for overshadowing the group's vocal talents, the quality and creativity of the music cannot be disputed.

Elsewhere there are no such problems, however, as the five-some's distinctive technique of lead vocal swapping is allowed to shine on three sophisticated funkers—the relentless 'Law of The Land', 'Plastic Man' and 'Ma'. Finally, a performance from falsetto lead Damon Harris closes the album on a sombre note with 'Hurry Tomorrow'.

A Seventies milestone, *Masterpiece* represents the ultimate combination of soul music's most successful male vocal group with one of its most innovative producers.

JACKIE WILSON

THE BEST OF
JACKIE WILSON
ACE, RE-RELEASED 1991

*W*HEN JACKIE WILSON'S MICROPHONE WENT ON THE BLINK DURING A FONDLY REMEM-BERED SHOW AT LONDON'S Rainbow Theatre in 1972, the man just went on singing regardless—and people hardly noticed, such was the strength and quality of his remarkable voice. The auditorium was only half-full but the atmosphere was magical on that wonderful night.

Jackie Wilson had a remarkable career which started in the rock 'n' roll era with 1957's 'Reet Petite'— a revived smash hit in the UK as late as the Eighties—and which carried Jackie through the golden age of soul to 1975 when he collapsed of a heart attack during a show at the Latin Casino in Camden, New Jersey, striking his head as he fell to the stage and incurring brain damage from which he never recovered. Jackie died on January 21, 1984, aged just 49, leaving behind a rich legacy of great recordings and a well-earned reputation as soul music's Mr Nice Guy.

It is said that the songwriting royalties from 'Reet Petite' helped Berry Gordy to set up Tamla Motown, and the influence of the association continued for some time, but Jackie was just as much at home with the near-blues of 'Doggin' Around' and the power-house, big band-accompanied 'Baby Workout' as he was with neo-Motown-styling items like 'Higher And Higher', 'Whispers (Getting Louder)' and '(I Get The) Sweetest Feeling', which remain heavily played golden oldies to this day.

Though the soul quotient was always very high, Jackie had the knack of stretching his musical expression beyond the confines of the black music genre to establish a truly international audience which recognized him not just as a soul brother *par excellence*, but as one of the greatest artists in popular music.

BOBBY WOMACK

THE POET
MOTOWN/BEVERLY GLEN, 1981

*B*OBBY EMERGED IN HIS OWN RIGHT AS A PROMINENT SINGER/SONGWRITER/PRODUCER IN THE SEVENTIES, BUT MANY FEEL that his greatest work can be found in the early Eighties recordings which comprise this classic album. Their refreshingly downhome, gritty musical approach, appearing in what was primarily an era of slick sophistication in black music, stunned fans when the album was released in 1981.

Bobby's natural gospel roots are evident in his rasping, intense vocals on cuts as varied as the rolling thumper 'So Many Sides Of You' and the swirling melodic ballad 'Just My Imagination', the rich country flavour of which is enhanced by some lilting slide guitar.

Elsewhere, Bobby's accomplished bluesy guitar-plucking adds a stinging edge to the flowing, tuneful 'Secrets' and a funky undercurrent to the stomping rhythms and burbling bass clarinet of the raucous 'Stand Up'.

However, it is the three marathon cuts that comprise the second side of the original vinyl album that constitute the set's real *tour de force*. The churchy acoustic piano and bluesy lilt of 'Games' hits a new level of emotion, setting the scene for 'If You Think You're Lonely Now', which builds from its introductory spoken dedication to "all the lovers tonight" into a whirlpool of gospel-flavoured intensity as the haunting title hook is repeated by a soulful backing choir alongside Bobby's testifying adlibs.

A similar vocal formula is followed for the slightly more sophisticated, orchestrated 'Where Do We Go From Here', Bobby's characteristic "preaching" and searing performance wringing every ounce of emotion out of the strong melody. 'Where Do We Go From Here' brings this milestone set to a suitably climactic end.

STEVIE WONDER

INNERVISIONS
TAMLA MOTOWN, 1973

*T*HE NEW-FOUND ARTIS-
TIC FREEDOM ACCORDED TO
BLACK MUSICIANS IN THE EARLY
SEVENTIES LED TO A GREAT DEAL OF
experimentation in differing musical
directions during this time. Stevie
Wonder was already an established
soul vocalist by 1970, but thereafter
a series of inventive albums earned
him the reputation of a universally
acclaimed singer, songwriter, multi-
instrumentalist, producer and "musical genius". Entirely written, produced, and largely played by Stevie
himself, *Innervisions* typically match-
es timeless personalized ballads with
irresistible up-tempo grooves, frequently reflecting the mood and
social awareness of his time.

Instrumentally, Stevie's fascination
with synthesizers is displayed in the
churning electronic funk rhythms of
'Higher Ground' and the jazz-tinged
chord progression of 'Too High'.
Meanwhile, acoustic piano and guitar enhance the natural beauty of
the reflective and introspective
'Visions', the haunting melodic qualities of which are retained for the
perceptive and meaningful 'All In
Love Is Fair'. Lyrically, on the
other hand, an angry social stand is
to be found on the pounding 'Living
For The City', its midway scenario
chillingly depicting the injustices of
black urban life
in Seventies
New York;
while the ethe-
real, multi-
tracked har-
monies of 'Jesus
Children Of
America' dis-
guise a serious
message of drug
abuse. On a
lighter note, the
conga-propelled
summery flavour
of 'Golden Lady'
hints at Latin
musical influ-
ences, which are later displayed
more obviously on the hot percussion and thumping piano of 'Don't
You Worry 'Bout A Thing', which
in turn leads us into 'He's Misstra
Know It All'—a tuneful mid-tempo
rippler whose instantly catchy piano
hook and infectious singalong feel
contrasts with Stevie's bitingly
scathing lyrics. This is an insight into
one of the twentieth century's true
musical geniuses.

CD listings

The following list contains the main albums by the artists and groups discussed earlier in the book. With the exception of compilations, the list focuses on albums that have charted in either the UK or USA and are available at the time of going to press. The listing is alphabetical and includes album title and year of original release on CD, record label and catalogue number, both in the USA and the UK. Compilations listed may not have charted, but are in most cases a reflection of an artist or group's best work currently available on CD.

ADEVA
Adeva
1989
UK: COOLTEMPO CCD-1719

STEVE ARRINGTON
NO CDs CURRENTLY AVAILABLE

ASHFORD AND SIMPSON
Solid *1985*
UK: CAPITOL CDP7464662

ATLANTIC STARR
All In The Name of Love *1987*
UK: WEA 925560 2

As The Band Turns
1985
UK: A&M CD 5019
The Best Of Atlantic Starr
1986
UK: A&M CDMID 152
Brilliance *1982*
JAPAN: A&M D20Y-4022
Classics: Atlantic Starr *1987*
US: A&M CD 2508

PATTI AUSTIN
Every Home Should Have One *1981*
UK: QWEST K256931

PHILIP BAILEY
Chinese Wall *1985*
UK: COLUMBIA CD26161

ANITA BAKER
Rapture *1986*
UK: ELEKTRA 9604442
US: ELEKTRA CD-60444
Giving You The Best That I Got *1988*
UK: ELEKTRA 9608272
US: ELEKTRA CD-60827
Compositions
1985
UK: ELEKTRA EKT72CD
US: ELEKTRA CD-60922
Songstress *1991*
UK: ELEKTRA 7559-61116-2
US: ELEKTRA 61116-2

REGINA BELLE
All By Myself *1987*
UK: COLUMBIA 4670172
US: COLUMBIA 40537
Stay With Me *1989*
UK: COLUMBIA DBS 465132-2
US: COLUMBIA 44367

GEORGE BENSON
20/20 *1985*
UK: WARNER BROS 925178 2
Breezin' *1976*
UK: WARNER BROS K256199
George Benson Collection *1981*
UK: WARNER BROS 7599-235772
Give Me The Night
1980
UK: WARNER BROS K256823
In Flight *1977*
UK: WARNER BROS 256327

In Your Eyes *1983*
UK: WARNER BROS 923744 2
Living Inside Your Love *1979*
UK: WARNER BROS K266085
Midnight Moods
1991
UK: TELSTAR TCD 2450
Tenderly *1989*
UK: WARNER BROS 925907 2
Twice The Love
1988
UK: WARNER BROS 925705 2
Weekend In L.A.
1978
JAPAN: WARNER BROS WPCP 3874
While The City Sleeps *1986*
UK: WARNER BROS 925475 2

GEORGE BENSON/EARL KLUGH
Collaboration *1987*
UK: WARNER BROS 925580 2

BOOKER T AND THE MGs
The Best Of Booker T And The MGs
1987
UK: LONDON FCD60004
Green Onions
1962
UK: LONDON/STAX 7567-82255-2
US: STAX 822 55-2
Hip Hug-Her *1967*
US: RHINO 71013-2
McLemore Avenue
1970
UK: STAX SXE 016

BOYZ II MEN
Cooleyhighharmony
1992
UK: MOTOWN ZD 72737
US: MOTOWN MOTD 6320

JOHNNY BRISTOL
NO CDs CURRENTLY AVAILABLE

BOBBY BROWN
Bobby *1992*
UK: MCA MCD 10695
US: MCAD 10417
Dance!...Ya Know It!
1989
UK: MCA DMCG6074
US: MCAD 6342
Don't Be Cruel
1988
UK: MCA DMCF3425
US: MCAD 42185

JAMES BROWN
20 Greatest Hits
1989
UK: MAINLINE 266202 2
Best Of James Brown (Godfather Of Soul)
1987
UK: K-TEL NCD3376
I Can't Stand Myself (When You Touch Me) *1968*
JAPAN: KING POCP 1853
Live At The Apollo
1963
UK: KING/POLYDOR 843479 2
Live At The Apollo Vol. 2
1968
UK: KING 823003 2

The Payback *1974*
UK: POLYDOR 314517 137-2
Sex Machine *1970*
UK: SUCCESS 2175 CD
Sex Machine And Other Soul Classics *1990*
US: POLYDOR 825714 2
Star Time *1991*
UK: POLYDOR PGR-849-108-2
The Very Best Of James Brown *1991*
UK: POLYDOR 845828 2

PEABO BRYSON
Born To Love *1983*
CANADA: CAPITOL C21Y-91329

CAMEO
Alligator Woman *1982*
JAPAN: MERCURY PHCR 6083
Cameosis *1980*
JAPAN: MERCURY PHCR 1093
Machismo *1988*
UK: CLUB 836002 2
She's Strange *1984*
UK: ATLANTA ARTISTS 814984-2
US: POLYGRAM 814984-2
Single Life *1985*
UK: CLUB 824546 2
Word Up *1986*
UK: CLUB/ATLANTA ARTISTS 830265-2
CANADA: POLYDOR 830265-2

CHANGE
The Glow Of Love *1980*
US: WARNER BROS 3438-2

CHIC
The Best Of Chic *1979*
JAPAN: ATLANTIC AMCY-119
C'Est Chic *1979*
JAPAN: ATLANTIC AMCY-117
Chic *1978*
JAPAN: ATLANTIC AMCY-116
Mega Chic (The Best Of Chic) *1990*
UK: WEA 2292417502
Real People *1980*
JAPAN: ATLANTIC AMCY-178
Risque *1979*
JAPAN: ATLANTIC AMCY-118

CHIC/SISTER SLEDGE
Freak Out *1987*
UK: TELSTAR 2292-41246-2

CHI-LITES
19 Greatest Hits *1992*
US: RHINO 70532-2
Best Of The Chi-Lites *1987*
UK: KENT CDKEN911
The Very Best Of The Chi-Lites *1991*
UK: MCI MCCD029

NATALIE COLE
Everlasting *1988*
UK: ELEKTRA 7559-61114-2
US: ELEKTRA 61114-2
Good To Be Back *1989*
UK: ELEKTRA 7559-61115-2
US: ELEKTRA 61115-2
Inseparable *1975*
US: CAPITOL CDP 7977692

The Soul Of Natalie Cole *1991*
UK: CAPITOL CDEST 2157
Unforgettable *1991*
UK: ELEKTRA 7559610492

COMMODORES
14 Greatest Hits *1987*
UK: MOTOWN ZD72421
US: MOTOWN MOTD 9039
Caught In The Act *1975*
UK: MOTOWN MOTD 5240
Commodores *1977*
US: MOTOWN MOTD-5222
Greatest Hits *1978*
US: MOTOWN MOTD 912
Heroes *1980*
US: MOTOWN MOTD 5353
Hot On The Tracks *1976*
UK: MOTOWN ZD72551
US: MOTOWN MOTD 8144
In The Pocket *1981*
UK: MOTOWN ZD72551
US: MOTOWN MOTD 8144
Live *1977*
UK: MOTOWN WD 72439
Midnight Magic *1979*
UK: MOTOWN ZD72455
US: MOTOWN MOTD 8114
Natural High *1978*
UK: MOTOWN ZD72455
Nightshift *1985*
UK: MOTOWN WD 72652

SAM COOKE
The Best Of Sam Cooke *1962*
US: RCA 3863-2

The Magic Of Sam Cooke *1991*
UK: MCI MCCD021
The Man And His Music *1986*
UK: RCA PD87127
US: RCA 7127-2
Sam Cooke *1958*
UK: GRAFFITI GRCD-04
Sam Cooke *1987*
UK: DEJA VU DVCD2095
Sam Cooke At The Copa *1965*
CANADA: ABKCO 2970-2

RANDY CRAWFORD
Abstract Emotions *1986*
UK: WARNER BROS 925423 2
The Love Songs *1987*
UK: WARNER BROS TCD2299
JAPAN: WARNER BROS WPCP 4554
Nightline *1983*
UK: WARNER BROS 923976 2
Now We May Begin *1980*
UK: WARNER BROS 7599-234212
Rich And Poor *1989*
UK: WARNER BROS K9260022
Secret Combination *1981*
UK: WARNER BROS K256904
Windsong *1982*
JAPAN: WARNER BROS WPCP 4367

WILL DOWNING
Come Together As One *1989*
UK: 4TH & BROADWAY

BRCD538
US: ISLAND 842348-2
A Dream Fulfilled *1991*
UK: 4TH & BROADWAY BRCD565
US: POLYGRAM 84278-2
Will Downing *1988*
UK: 4TH & BROADWAY BRCD518
US: ISLAND 842689-2

DRIFTERS
20 Greatest Hits *1988*
UK: SPECTRUM SPEC85006
The Drifters *1990*
UK: TELSTAR TCD2373

EARTH WIND AND FIRE
All 'N' All *1977*
JAPAN: SONY SRCS 6114
The Best Of Earth Wind And Fire Vol. 1 *1978*
UK: COLUMBIA CD32536
The Collection *1986*
UK: SONY 4658882
Electric Universe *1984*
JAPAN: SONY SRCS 6116
Faces *1980*
US: COLUMBIA CGK 36795
Gratitude *1975*
UK: COLUMBIA CD88160
US: COLUMBIA 33694
Head To The Sky *1973*
JAPAN: SONY SRCS 6109
I Am *1979*
UK: COLUMBIA CD 86084

Open Our Eyes *1974*
US: Sony 32712

Powerlight *1983*
UK: Columbia CDCBS25120

Raise *1981*
UK: Columbia 467388 2

Spirit *1976*
Japan: Sony SRCS 6113

That's The Way Of The World *1975*
UK: Columbia CD80575

Touch The World *1987*
UK: Columbia 4604092

The Very Best Of Earth Wind And Fire *1988*
UK: Columbia 463200–2

The Very Best Of Earth Wind And Fire Vol. 2 *1988*
UK: Arcade ADEHCD821/1

EN VOGUE

Born To Sing *1990*
UK: Atlantic 7567820842
US: Atlantic 82084–2

Funky Divas *1992*
UK: East West 7567-92121-2

ROBERTA FLACK

The Best of Roberta Flack *1978*
UK: WEA 250840

Blue Lights In The Basement *1978*
US: Atlantic 19149–2

Chapter Two *1970*
Japan: Atlantic 18P2 3080

Feel Like Makin' Love *1975*
US: Atlantic 7803332

First Take *1972*
Japan: Atlantic 18P2 3079

Killing Me Softly *1973*
Japan: Atlantic 2-19154

Quiet Fire *1971*
Japan: Atlantic 18P2 3081

ROBERTA FLACK/DONNY HATHAWAY

Roberta Flack And Donny Hathaway *1980*
US: Atlantic 7216-2

Roberta Flack featuring Donny Hathaway *1980*
Japan: Atlantic 18P2-3087

FOUR TOPS

Anthology *1983*
UK: Motown WD 72528
US: Motown MOTD 2809

Four Tops Live! *1967*
US: Motown MOTD 5258

Four Tops On Top *1966*
US: Motown MOTD 5444

Four Tops Second Album *1966*
UK: Motown ZD72491
US: Motown MOTD 8127

Greatest Hits *1967*
UK: Motown WD72280
US: Motown MOTD 5209

Keeper Of The Castle *1972*
US: Dunhill MOTD 5428

Reach Out *1967*
UK: Motown WD72067
US: Motown MOTD 5149

Still Waters Run Deep *1970*
UK: Motown WD72734
US: Motown MOTD 5224

Their Greatest Hits *1990*
UK: Telstar TCD2437

Tonight! *1981*
UK: Casablanca 800049 2

ARETHA FRANKLIN

20 Greatest Hits *1987*
UK: WEA 2411352

Amazing Grace *1972*
US: Atlantic 906-2

Aretha *1986*
UK: Arista 258883
US: Arista ARCD 8556

Aretha Arrives *1967*
Japan: Atlantic AMCY-44

Aretha Franklin—30 Greatest Hits *1986*
UK: Atlantic 78 1668-2

Aretha Live At Fillmore West *1971*
UK: Atlantic MFCD 820

Aretha Now *1971*
Japan: Atlantic 2OP2-2373

Aretha's Gold *1969*
US: Atlantic 82272

Collection *1987*
UK: Castle CCSCD 152

I Never Loved A Man The Way I Love You *1967*
Japan: Atlantic 2OP2-2364

Jump To It *1982*
UK: Arista 259060

Lady Soul *1968*
UK: Atlantic K7818182

Love All The Hurt Away *1981*
UK: Arista 253913

Spirit In The Dark *1970*
Japan: Atlantic AMCY-66

Through The Storm *1989*
UK: Arista 259842
US: Arista ARCD 8572

Who's Zoomin' Who? *1986*
UK: Arista 259053
US: Arista ARCD 8286

MARVIN GAYE

The Best Of Marvin Gaye *1976*
UK: Motown 72612

Dream Of A Lifetime *1985*
UK: Epic 982591-2

I Want You *1976*
UK: Motown ZD72457
US: Motown MOTD 8110

Let's Get It On *1973*
UK: Motown ZD72085
US: Motown MOTD 5192

Love Songs *1990*
UK: Telstar TCD 2331

M.P.G. *1969*
UK: Tamla MOTD 5125

Marvin Gaye *1990*
UK: Telstar TCD2427

Marvin Gaye Live! *1974*
UK: Tamla WD 72086
US: Motown MOTD 5181

Marvin Gaye Live At The London Palladium *1977*
UK: Tamla ZD72213
US: Motown MOTD 5259

Midnight Love *1982*
UK: Columbia 461017 2
US: Columbia 38197

Trouble Man *1973*
UK: Tamla ZD72500
US: Motown MOTD 8136

What's Going On *1971*
UK: Tamla ZD72611
US: Motown MOTD 5339

MARVIN GAYE AND TAMMI TERRELL

Greatest Hits *1970*
UK: Motown WD 72103
US: Motown MOTD 5225

GLORIA GAYNOR

Collection *1992*
UK: Castle CCSCD340

Gloria Gaynor's Greatest Hits *1988*
UK: Polydor 833 433-2

Love Tracks *1979*
Japan: Polydor POCP-2183

The Power Of Gloria Gaynor *1986*
UK: Stylus SMD618

AL GREEN

Al *1992*
UK: MasterCuts AGREECD 1

Al Green Explores Your Mind *1974*
UK: Hi HIUKCD413
US: Motown MOTD 5287

Al Green Is Love
1975
UK: HI MIUKCD 114
US: MOTOWN MOTD 8148

Al Green's Greatest Hits
1975
UK: LONDON HIUKCD425

Call Me 1973
UK: HI HIUKCD111

Green Is Blues 1973
UK: HI HIUKCD106

Hi Life—The Best Of Al Green 1988
UK: K-TEL NCD3420

I'm Still In Love With You 1972
UK: HI HIUKCD111
US: MOTOWN MOTD 5284

Let's Stay Together
1972
UK: HI HIUKCD405
US: MOTOWN MOTD 5290

Livin' For You 1974
UK: HI HIUKCD113

DONNY HATHAWAY
Donny Hathaway Live 1972
JAPAN: ATCO 18P2-3090

ISAAC HAYES
Black Moses 1971
UK: STAX CDSXE2033

Hot Buttered Soul
1969
UK: ENTERPRISE CDSXE005
US: ENTERPRISE SCD 4114

The Isaac Hayes Movement 1970
UK: ENTERPRISE CDSXE025

Isaac's Moods (The Best Of)
1988
UK: STAX/ACE CDSX011

Joy 1973
UK: ENTERPRISE CDSXE047
US: ENTERPRISE SCD 8530

Live At The Sahara Tahoe 1973
UK: ENTERPRISE CDSXE2053
US: ENTERPRISE SCD 88004

Shaft 1971
UK: POLYDOR CDSXD-021

To Be Continued
1970
UK: ENTERPRISE CDSXE030

HEATWAVE
Gangsters Of The Groove 1991
UK: INTERCORD 845.550

Powercuts—All Their Hottest Hits
1990
UK: EPIC468921 2

Too Hot Too Handle 1977
US: GTO EK34761

WHITNEY HOUSTON
I'm Your Baby Tonight
1990
UK: ARISTA 261039
US: ARISTA ARCD 8616

Whitney 1987
UK: ARISTA 258141
US: ARISTA ARCD 8616

Whitney Houston
1985
UK: ARISTA 610359
US: ARISTA ARCD 8212

PHYLLIS HYMAN
Living All Alone
1986
UK: PIR CDP 7464222

Under Her Spell
1989
UK: ARISTA 260620
US: ARISTA ARCD 8609

IMPRESSIONS
The Definitive Impressions 1989
UK: ACE CDKEND923

JAMES INGRAM
It's Your Night
1984
UK: QWEST 9239702

Never Felt So Good
1986
UK: QWEST 9254242

ISLEY BROTHERS
3+3 1973
UK: T-NECK 9826512
US: SONY MUSIC 32453

Go For Your Guns
1977
US: EPIC ZK34432

Grand Slam 1981
JAPAN: T-NECK SRCS 6124

Greatest Hits 1986
UK: TELSTAR TCD2306

The Heat Is On 1975
US: T-NECK ZK 33536

This Old Heart Of Mine 1968
UK: MOTOWN 3746351282
US: MOTOWN MOTD 5128

Winner Takes All
1979
US: T-NECK ZGK 36077

FREDDIE JACKSON
Do Me Again
1990
US: CAPITOL C21S 92217

Don't Let Love Slip Away
1988
UK: EMI CZ 401
US: CAPITOL C21Y 48987

Just Like The First Time 1986
UK: EMI CZ 118

Rock Me Tonight
1985
US: CAPITOL CDP746170 2

JANET JACKSON
Control 1986
UK: A&M CDA5106
US: A&M CD 3905

Control—The Remixes
1987
UK: A&M CDMID149

Rhythm Nation 1814
1989
UK: A&M CDA3920

JERMAINE JACKSON
Greatest Hits And Rare Classics 1991
UK: MOTOWN WD72706

Let's Get Serious
1980
US: MOTOWN 3746353542

MICHAEL JACKSON
Bad 1987
UK: EPIC 4502902

Ben 1972
UK: MOTOWN WD72069
US: MOTOWN MOTD 5153

Best Of Michael Jackson 1981
UK: MOTOWN WD72063
US: MOTOWN MOTD 5194

Dangerous 1991
UK: EPIC 465802 2
US: EPIC 45400

Farewell My Summer Love 1984
UK: MOTOWN WD72630

Got To Be There
1972
UK: MOTOWN WD72068
US: MOTOWN MOTD 5416

The Michael Jackson Mix
1987
UK: STYLUS SMD745

Off The Wall 1979
UK: EPIC CD83468

One Day In Your Life 1981
US: MOTOWN 3746353522

Thriller 1982
UK: EPIC CD 85930

JACKSONS/ JACKSON FIVE
2300 Jackson Street
1989
UK: EPIC 460579-2
US: EPIC 40911

ABC 1970
UK: MOTOWN ZD72483
US: MOTOWN MOTD 8119

Anthology—The Jackson Five
1992
UK: MOTOWN WD 72529
US: MOTOWN 3746308682

Destiny 1979
UK: EPIC CD32365

**Diana Ross Presents
The Jackson Five**
1970
UK: MOTOWN ZD72483
US: MOTOWN MOTD 5129
Goin' Places *1977*
UK: EPIC 4688762
**The Greatest Hits Of
The Jackson Five**
1988
UK: MOTOWN WD72087
US: MOTOWN MOTD 5201
**Jackson Five
Greatest Hits** *1972*
UK: MOTOWN WD72087
US: MOTOWN MOTD 5201
The Jacksons *1977*
UK: EPIC 9827382
Jacksons Live *1981*
US: EPIC EGK 37545
Maybe Tomorrow
1971
US: MOTOWN 3746352282
Third Album *1970*
US: MOTOWN 3746351572
Triumph *1980*
UK: EPIC 9866402
Victory *1984*
UK: EPIC CD86303

RICK JAMES
Cold Blooded *1983*
US: GORDY MOTD 5468
Come Get It *1978*
US: GORDY 3746352632
**Reflections Of Rick
James** *1984*
UK: GORDY ZD72174
US: GORDY 6095
Street Songs *1981*
UK: GORDY ZD72474
US: GORDY MOTD 5405

Throwin' Down
1982
UK: GORDY ZD72474

AL JARREAU
Breakin' Away *1981*
UK: WARNER BROS 925425 2
High Crime *1984*
UK: WARNER BROS 250807 2
Jarreau *1983*
UK: WARNER BROS U00702
L Is For Lover *1986*
UK: WARNER BROS 253080 2
This Time *1980*
US: WARNER BROS 3434-2

BROTHERS JOHNSON
Blam!! *1978*
JAPAN: CANYON D28Y-3239
**Classics (Brothers
Johnson)** *1985*
UK: A&M CDA2509
Light Up The Night
1980
JAPAN: A&M D28Y-3240
Look Out For No. 1
1976
JAPAN: CANYON D28Y-3238
Right On Time *1977*
JAPAN: CANYON D32Y-3111

GLENN JONES
Best Of Glenn Jones
1991
US: JIVE 01241-41503-2
Glenn Jones *1987*
UK: JIVE CHIP-51
US: NOVUS 1062-2

EDDIE KENDRICKS
At His Best *1978*
US: MOTOWN 37463 54812

CHAKA KHAN
Chaka *1978*
JAPAN: WARNER BROS
18P2-2672
Destiny *1986*
UK: WARNER BROS 925425 2
I Feel For You *1984*
UK: WARNER BROS 925162 2
**Life Is A Dance—
The Remix Project**
1989
UK: WARNER BROS 925946 2
**What Cha' Gonna
Do For Me** *1981*
JAPAN: WARNER BROS
18P2-2672

BEN E. KING
NO CDS CURRENTLY AVAILABLE

EVELYN KING
**Essential Works Of
Evelyn "Champagne"
King** *1992*
UK: RCA 7432110703 24

**GLADYS KNIGHT AND
THE PIPS**
2nd Anniversary
1975
JAPAN: TEICHIKU 220N-101
All Our Love
1988
UK: MCA DMCL1895
**The Best of Gladys
Knight And The
Pips** *1976*
UK: BUDDAH 472038-2
**Best Of Gladys
Knight And The
Pips** *1992*
UK: PICKWICK 9827352

**The Best Of Gladys
Knight And The
Pips** *1991*
UK: COLUMBIA 472038 2
Claudine *1974*
UK: BUDDAH NEXCD206
**The Collection—20
Greatest Hits** *1984*
UK: CASTLE CCSD-206
I Feel A Song *1975*
UK: BUDDAH NEXCD192
**If I Were Your
Woman** *1971*
US: SOUL 3746353882
Imagination *1973*
UK: BUDDAH NEXCD192
Neither One Of Us
1973
UK: SOUL ZD72461
US: MOTOWN MOTD 8108
The Singles Album
1989
UK: POLYGRAM 842003 2
Still Together *1977*
UK: BUDDAH NEXCD206
Visions *1983*
UK: COLUMBIA 902119 2

KOOL AND THE GANG
Anthology *1991*
UK: CONNOISSEUR
VSOPCD 168
As One *1982*
UK: DE-LITE 822535 2
Celebrate! *1980*
US: POLYGRAM 822538-2
Emergency *1984*
UK: DE-LITE 822943 2
Forever
1985
UK: DE-LITE 830398 2

In The Heart *1984*
UK: DE-LITE DECD 8508
Kool Love *1990*
UK: TELSTAR TCD2435
Ladies' Night
1979
UK: DE-LITE 822537 2
**The Singles
Collection** *1988*
UK: DE-LITE 836 636 2
Something Special
1981
UK: DE-LITE 822534 2

PATTI LABELLE
Best Of Patti Labelle
1986
JAPAN: EPIC 28 8P 1087
The Winner In You
1986
UK: MCA 31159
US: MCA MCAD 31159

LEVERT
The Big Throwdown
1987
JAPAN: ATLANTIC 32XD 894

JOHNNY MATHIS
**16 Most Requested
Songs** *1990*
UK: COLUMBIA CD 57059
Celebration *1981*
UK: SONY MUSIC 467452-2
Friends In Love *1982*
US: SONY MUSIC 37748
Heavenly *1991*
UK: COLUMBIA MFCD825
**The Johnny Mathis
Collection**
1977
UK: CASTLE CCSCS 343

136

Merry Christmas
1991
UK: COLUMBIA CD 57039
US: SONY 8021
A Special Part Of Me *1984*
UK: COLUMBIA CD25475
Tears And Laughter *1980*
UK: COLUMBIA 4683072

JOHNNY MATHIS AND NATALIE COLE
A Tribute To Nat King Cole *1983*
UK: COLUMBIA 469437

JOHNNY MATHIS AND DENIECE WILLIAMS
That's What Friends Are For *1978*
UK: COLUMBIA 902124 2

CURTIS MAYFIELD
A Man Like Curtis *1992*
UK: MCI MUSCD 007
Superfly *1973*
UK: CURTOM CDCUR2002

MAZE FEATURING FRANKIE BEVERLY
Lifelines—Volume 1 *1989*
UK: CAPITOL CDEST2111
US: CAPITOL C21Y92810
Live In Los Angeles *1986*
UK: CAPITOL CDP 746369 2
Live In New Orleans *1981*
UK: CAPITOL CDP 746659

Silky Soul *1989*
UK: WARNER BROS K9258022
US: WEA CD 28802

HAROLD MELVIN
Satisfaction Guaranteed—The Best Of Harold Melvin *1992*
UK: NICE PRICE472039 2
Wake Up Everybody *1975*
US: PIR ZK 33808

MIDNIGHT STAR
The Best Of Midnight Star *1992*
UK: SOLAR 468920 2
Headlines *1986*
UK: SOLAR DMCF3322
No Parking On The Dancefloor *1983*
JAPAN: SOLAR CSCS 5288

STEPHANIE MILLS
The Collection *1992*
UK: CASTLE CCSCD337
If I Were Your Woman *1987*
UK: MCA DMCF3385
US: MCA MCAD 5996
In My Life *1987*
UK: CASABLANCA 832519-2

BILLY OCEAN
Greatest Hits *1989*
UK: JIVE BOCD 1
Love Zone *1986*
UK: JIVE CHIP 35
US: NOVUS 1223-2

Suddenly *1984*
UK: JIVE CHIP 12
Tear Down These Walls *1988*
UK: JIVE CHIP 57
US: NOVUS 1224-2

O'JAYS
Collectors' Items *1977*
US: PIR 468922 2
Family Reunion *1975*
US: PIR ZK 33807
Identify Yourself *1979*
JAPAN: PIR ALCB 629
Message In The Music *1976*
JAPAN: PIR ALCB 628
Reflections In Gold (1973–82) *1988*
UK: CHARLY CDCHARLY 109
Ship Ahoy *1974*
US: PIR ZK 32408
So Full of Love *1978*
JAPAN: PIR ALCB 629

OMAR
There's Nothing Like This *1990*
UK: TALKING LOUD 510021 2

ALEXANDER O'NEAL
Alexander O'Neal *1985*
UK: TABU460187 2
All True Man *1991*
UK: TABU 465882 2
US: TABU 45349

The Greatest Hits Of Alexander O'Neal *1992*
UK: TABU 471714 2
Hearsay *1987*
UK: TABU 450936 2
Hearsay/All Mixed Up *1987*
UK: TABU 466123 2
US: COLUMBIA ZK-44492
My Gift To You *1988*
UK: TABU 463152 2
US: SONY MUSIC 45016

JEFFREY OSBORNE
Don't Stop *1984*
UK: A&M CDA5017
Emotional *1986*
UK: A&M CDA5103
Stay With Me Tonight *1984*
UK: A&M CDA64940

MICA PARIS
Contribution *1990*
UK: 4TH & BROADWAY BRCD-558
US: POLYGRAM 846814-2
So Good *1988*
UK: 4TH & BROADWAY BRCD X525
US: ISLAND 842-497-2

RAY PARKER
After Dark *1987*
UK: WEA 924124 2
The Other Woman *1982*
JAPAN: ARISTA BVCA 2027

RAY PARKER Jr. (RAYDIO)
Raydio *1978*
JAPAN: ARISTA BVCA 2023

RAY PARKER AND RAYDIO
Best Of Ray Parker Jnr with Raydio *1989*
UK: ARIOLA 260365
Two Places At The Same Time *1980*
JAPAN: ARISTA BVCA 2025
A Woman Needs Love *1981*
JAPAN: ARISTA BVCA 2026

DAVID PEASTON
Introducing David Peaston *1989*
UK: GEFFEN K9242282

TEDDY PENDERGRASS
Joy *1988*
UK: ELEKTRA 9607752
Love Language *1984*
UK: ASYLUM 960317 2
Teddy *1979*
JAPAN: PIR ALCB 627
Teddy Pendergrass *1977*
JAPAN: PIR ALCB 626
Teddy Pendergrass Greatest Hits *1982*
US: PIR ZK39252
TP *1980*
JAPAN: PIR ALCB 627

WILSON PICKETT

The Best Of Wilson Pickett 1968
UK: International 781283-2

The Best Of Wilson Pickett 1987
UK: Atlantic 781737 2

The Exciting Wilson Pickett 1966
Japan: Atlantic 20P2-2372

POINTER SISTERS

Black And White 1981
UK: Planet ND89378

Break Out 1984
UK: Planet ND90206

Contact 1985
UK: RCA ND90089

Jump–The Best Of The Pointer Sisters 1989
UK: RCA PD90319

The Pointer Sisters 1973
UK: Ariola 260471

PRINCE

1999 1982
UK: Warner Bros 923720 2

Around The World In A Day 1985
UK: Warner Bros 925 286 2

Batman 1989
UK: Warner Bros 925 936 2

Controversy 1981
UK: Warner Bros K256950

Diamonds And Pearls 1991
UK: Warner Bros 7599253792

Get Off 1991
UK: Warner Bros 9401380

Graffiti Bridge 1990
UK: Warner Bros 759 927 4932

Lovesexy 1988
UK: Warner Bros 925 720 2

Parade 1986
UK: Warner Bros 925 395 2

Prince 1979
UK: Warner Bros K26577 2

Purple Rain 1984
UK: Warner Bros 925 110 2

Sign O' The Times 1987
UK: Warner Bros 925 577 2

OTIS REDDING

Dock Of The Bay 1968
UK: Stax 2411172
US: Stax 80254-2

Dock Of The Bay (The Definitive Collection) 1987
UK: Atlantic 241118 2

Great Soul Ballads 1966
UK: ATCO 7567-91706-2

Immortal Otis Redding 1968
US: Atlantic 80270-2

Otis Blue 1966
US: Atlantic 7567-80318-2

Otis Redding Live In Europe 1967
Japan: Volt 20P2-2363

Otis Redding's Dictionary Of Soul 1967
UK: Atlantic ATCO 7567-917072

Pain In My Heart 1967
US: Atlantic 780253-2

Soul Album 1966
UK: Atlantic ATCO 7567-91705-2
US: Atlantic 91705-2

OTIS REDDING AND CARLA THOMAS

King And Queen 1967
UK: Atlantic 7567 82256-2

LIONEL RICHIE

Back To Front 1992
UK: Motown 530 018-2
US: Motown MOTD 6338

Can't Slow Down 1983
UK: Motown ZD 72020
US: Motown MOTD 6059

Dancing On The Ceiling 1986
UK: Motown ZD 72412
US: Motown MOTD 6158

Lionel Richie 1982
UK: Motown ZD 72017
US: Motown MOTD 6007

MINNIE RIPERTON

The Best Of Minnie Riperton 1989
UK: Capitol CDP7917842

Love Lives Forever 1980
Japan: Capitol TOCP 6944

Minnie 1979
Japan: Capitol T0CP-6945

SMOKEY ROBINSON

Being With You 1981
US: Motown 3746353492

Blame It On Love And All The Great Hits 1991
UK: Motown WD72542
US: Motown MOTD 5401

One Heartbeat 1987
UK: Motown ZD72580

A Quiet Storm 1975
US: Tamla 3746351972

Where There's Smoke 1980
US: Tamla 3746352672

Yes It's You Lady 1982
UK: Tamla ZD72580

ROSE ROYCE

Car Wash 1976
UK: MCA MCD 18224

Greatest Hits 1980
UK: Atlantic 923457 2

DIANA ROSS

All The Great Hits 1981
US: Motown MOTD 960

An Evening With Diana Ross 1977
US: Motown MOTD 5268

Baby It's Me 1977
US: Motown MOTD 5434

The Boss 1979
UK: Motown WD 72095
US: Motown MOTD 5198

Diana 1971
UK: Motown WD72430
US: Motown MOTD 5383

Diana 1980
UK: Motown ZD72470

Diana Ross 1970
US: Motown 3746351352

Diana Ross 1976
UK: Motown WD72375
US: Motown MOTD 5294

Diana Ross 1982
UK: Motown WD 72375
US: Motown MOTD 5294

Eaten Alive 1985
UK: Capitol CDP7461842
US: RCA 5009-2

The Force Behind The Power 1991
UK: EMI CDEMD1023

Greatest Hits 1972
UK: Motown WD 72478
US: Motown MOTD 869

Greatest Hits Live 1989
UK: EMI CDEMCD1001

I'm Still Waiting 1971
UK: Motown ZD 72716

I'm Still Waiting And The Greatest Hits 1990
UK: Motown ZD72716

Lady Sings The Blues 1972
UK: Motown WD72610

Portrait 1983
UK: Telstar TCD2238AR3

**Red Hot Rhythm 'N'
Blues** *1987*
UK: EMI CDP7467872
US: RCA 6388-2
Ross *1983*
JAPAN: CAPITOL/RCA
TOCP-6345
Silk Electric *1982*
US: RCA 4384-2
Swept Away *1984*
UK: EMI CDP 746053-2
**Touch Me In The
Morning** *1973*
UK: MOTOWN WD72074
US: MOTOWN MOTD 5163
**Why Do Falls Fool
In Love**
1981
UK: CAPITOL/RCA CDFA3186
US: EMI CDP 746 023-2
Workin' Overtime
1989
UK: EMI CD EMD-1009
US: MOTOWN MOTD 6274

**DIANA ROSS AND
MARVIN GAYE**
Diana And Marvin
1974
UK: MOTOWN WD 72066
US: MOTOWN MOTD 5124

**DIANA ROSS AND THE
SUPREMES WITH THE
TEMPTATIONS**
**Diana Ross Joins
The Temptations**
1986
UK: MOTOWN ZD72502
US: MOTOWN MOTD 8138
TCB *1969*
US: MOTOWN MOTD 5171

Together *1970*
UK: MOTOWN ZD72502
US: MOTOWN MOTD 8138

DAVID RUFFIN
At His Best *1992*
US: MOTOWN 3746352112

JIMMY RUFFIN
**Greatest Motown
Hits** *1989*
UK: MOTOWN WD72654

**RUFUS AND CHAKA
KHAN**
Ask Rufus *1977*
US: ABC MCAD-10449
Rags To Rufus
1974
US: ABC MCAD 31365
**Rufus Featuring
Chaka Khan**
1975
US: ABC MCAD-31373
Rufusized *1975*
US: ABC MCAD 10236
**Stompin' At The
Savoy** *1984*
JAPAN: WARNER BROS
WPCP 4885-6

SADE
Diamond Life
1984
UK: EPIC CD26044
Love Deluxe *1992*
UK: EPIC 472626 2
Promise *1985*
UK: EPIC 465575 2
Stronger Than Pride
1988
UK: EPIC 460497 2

SAM AND DAVE
**The Best Of Sam
And Dave** *1978*
UK: ATLANTIC 7812792
Double Dynamite
1967
US: ATLANTIC 80305-2
Hold On I'm Comin'
1967
US: ATLANTIC 7567-80255-2
Soul Man *1968*
UK: SUCCESS 2215-CD

SHALAMAR
Friends *1982*
UK: SOLAR 252345
Greatest Hits *1982*
UK: MCA DSMR 8615
**Here It Is—The Best
Of Shalamar**
1992
UK: SOLAR 472040 2
The Look *1983*
JAPAN: SOLAR CSCS 5286

SISTER SLEDGE
NO CDS CURRENTLY AVAILABLE
(SEE ALSO CHIC/SISTER
SLEDGE)

**SLY AND THE FAMILY
STONE**
**The Best Of Sly And
The Family Stone**
1992
UK: EPIC 471758 2
Fresh *1973*
UK: EDSEL EDCD 232
US: SONY 32134
Greatest Hits *1970*
UK: EPIC 4625242
US: EPIC 30325

Small Talk *1974*
JAPAN: EPIC ESCA 5384
Stand! *1969*
JAPAN: EPIC ESCA 5383
**There's A Riot Goin'
On** *1971*
UK: EPIC EDCD165

SOUL II SOUL
**Club Classics Vol. 1:
Keep On Movin'**
1989
UK: VIRGIN/10 RECORDS
DIXCD 82
US: VIRGIN/10 RECORDS
V21S-86122
**Vol. 2: 1990—A New
Decade** *1990*
UK: VIRGIN/10 RECORDS
DIXCD 90
US: VIRGIN/10 RECORDS
V21Z-86165

LISA STANSFIELD
Affection *1989*
UK: ARISTA 260379
Real Love *1991*
UK: ARISTA 262300
US: ARISTA ARCD 18679

STYLISTICS
**The Best Of The
Stylistics** *1975*
US: AMHERST 9743
**The Best Of The
Stylistics 1990**
1990
UK: MERCURY 842936 2
**The Greatest Hits Of
The Stylistics**
1992
UK: MERCURY 512 985-2

Rockin' Roll Baby
1974
JAPAN: AVCO VICP 2038
**Round 2: The
Stylistics** *1973*
JAPAN: AVCO VICP 2037
The Stylistics *1972*
JAPAN: AVCO VICP 2036
Thank You Baby
1975
JAPAN: AVCO VICP 2039

DONNA SUMMER
**Another Place And
Time** *1989*
UK: WARNER BROS 255976 2
Bad Girls *1979*
UK: CASABLANCA 822557 2
**The Best Of Donna
Summer** *1990*
UK: WARNER BROS
903172 9092
Cats Without Claws
1984
UK: WARNER BROS 25080 62
Donna Summer
1982
UK: WARNER BROS K299163
**Four Seasons Of
Love** *1976*
US: CASABLANCA 826 236-2
**I Remember
Yesterday** *1977*
US: CASABLANCA 826 237-2
**Love To Love You
Baby** *1975*
US: POLYGRAM 822 792-2
A Love Trilogy
1976
US: POLYGRAM 822793
On The Radio *1979*
UK: CASABLANCA 822558 2

Once Upon A Time
1977
UK: CASABLANCA 826238 2
She Works Hard For The Money
1983
US: MERCURY 812265 2

SUPREMES
A Bit Of Liverpool
1965
US: MOTOWN 3746354292
Cream Of The Crop
1969
UK: MOTOWN ZD72496
US: MOTOWN MOTD 5435
Greatest Hits *1967*
UK: MOTOWN ZD72493
Greatest Hits And Rare Classics
1991
UK: MOTOWN WD72773
I Hear A Symphony
1966
US: MOTOWN 3746351472
Let The Sun Shine In *1969*
UK: MOTOWN ZD72496
US: MOTOWN MOTD 8132
Love Child *1969*
UK: MOTOWN ZD72485
US: MOTOWN MOTD 8121
Love Supreme *1989*
UK: MOTOWN ZD72701
Meet The Supremes
1964
US: MOTOWN MOTD 5223
More Hits By The Supremes
1865
UK: MOTOWN WD72117
US: MOTOWN MOTD 5440

Reflections
1968
US: MOTOWN MOTD 5494
Right On *1970*
US: MOTOWN 3746354422
Supremes A Go-Go
1966
UK: MOTOWN ZD72485
US: MOTOWN MOTD 8121
The Supremes At The Copa
1965
US: MOTOWN 3746351622
Supremes Sing Motown *1967*
US: MOTOWN MOTD 5371
Supremes Sing Rodgers And Hart
1967
UK: MOTOWN WD72594
TCB *1969*
US: MOTOWN MOTD 5171
Touch *1971*
UK: MOTOWN MOTD 5447
US: MOTOWN MOTD 72742 UK
Where Did Our Love Go
1964
UK: MOTOWN WD72735
US: MOTOWN MOTD 5270

SUPREMES AND THE FOUR TOPS
Magnificent Seven
1971
US: MOTOWN MOTD 5123
The Best Of The Supremes And The Four Tops *1991*
UK: MOTOWN WD72776
US: MOTOWN MOTD 5491

KEITH SWEAT
I'll Give All My Love To You *1990*
UK: VINTERTAINMENT 7559608612
Make It Last Forever *1988*
UK: ELEKTRA 9607632

SYLVESTER
Star—Best Of Sylvester *1989*
UK: ACE CDSEW007

TEMPTATIONS
All Directions *1973*
UK: MOTOWN WD72321
US: MOTOWN MOTD 5417
Anthology Vols. 1 & 2 *1989*
UK: MOTOWN WD72525
US: MOTOWN MOTD 2782
Cloud Nine *1969*
UK: MOTOWN ZD72460
US: MOTOWN MOTD 8116
Getting Ready *1966*
US: MOTOWN 3746353732
Greatest Hits Vol. 2
1970
UK: MOTOWN WD72647
US: MOTOWN MOTD 5412
Live At The Copa
1969
UK: GORDY ZD72501
US: MOTOWN MOTD 8137
Masterpiece *1973*
UK: MOTOWN WD72076
US: MOTOWN MOTD 5144
Psychedelic Shack
1970
UK: MOTOWN ZD72486
US: MOTOWN MOTD 8122

Puzzle People *1970*
UK: MOTOWN ZD72460
US: MOTOWN MOTD 5172
Sky's The Limit *1971*
UK: GORDY WD72743
US: MOTOWN MOTD 5474
Solid Rock *1972*
US: MOTOWN 3746354802
A Song For You
1975
UK: GORDY ZD72499
US: MOTOWN MOTD 5272
The Temptations Sing Smokey
1965
US: GORDY 374635052
Temptations Greatest Hits *1967*
UK: MOTOWN WD72646
US: MOTOWN MOTD 5411
Temptations Live
19647
US: MOTOWN 3746354992
The Temptations In A Mellow Mood
1968
US: GORDY 3746352352
Temptations With A Lot Of Soul
1967
UK: MOTOWN ZD72501
US: MOTOWN MOTD 8137
Together *1970*
UK: MOTOWN ZD72502
US: MOTOWN MOTD 8138
Truly For You
1984
UK: MOTOWN WD76244
US: MOTOWN MOTD 6119
Wish It Would Rain
1968
US: GORDY 3746352762

THREE DEGREES
The Best Of The Three Degrees *1979*
UK: CONNOISSEUR VSOP CD 149

TINA TURNER
Break Every Rule
1986
US: CAPITOL CDP7463232
Foreign Affair
1989
UK: CAPITOL CDEST-2103
US: CAPITOL C21S 91873
Live In Europe
1988
UK: CAPITOL CDS790126 2
US: CAPITOL C22V 90126
Private Dancer
1984
UK: CAPITOL CDP7460412
US: CAPITOL C21Y 46041
Simply The Best
1991
UK: CAPITOL CDESTV1
US: CAPITOL C2TT 97152

LUTHER VANDROSS
Any Love
1988
UK: EPIC CDLUTH11
Best Of Luther Vandross—Best Of Love *1989*
UK: EPIC 465801 2
US: EPIC E2K45320
Busy Body *1984*
UK: EPIC 460183-2
Forever For Always For Love
1982
UK: EPIC 4630012

Give Me The Reason
1986
UK: EPIC 450134 2
Never Too Much
1981
UK: EPIC CD 32807
US: EPIC 37451
The Night I Fell In Love *1985*
UK: EPIC CD 26387
US: EPIC WEK 39822
Power Of Love *1991*
UK: EPIC 468012 2
US: COLUMBIA 46789

DIONNE WARWICK
The 25th Anniversary Collection *1988*
UK: PICKWICK PWKS512
The Collection
1983
UK: ARISTA CDTRACK004
Dionne *1979*
US: ARISTA ARCD 8295
Friends *1986*
UK: ARISTA 259652
Heartbreaker
1982
UK: ARISTA 258719
The Love Songs
1990
UK: ARISTA 260441
No Night So Long
1980
JAPAN: ARISTA A32D56
So Amazing
1983
UK: ARISTA 1610099
Without Your Love
1985
UK: ARISTA 258553

WHISPERS
Imagination *1981*
JAPAN: SOLAR CSCS 5284
In The Mood *1990*
US: SOLAR ZK 75321
Just Gets Better With Time *1987*
UK: SOLAR DMCF3381

BARRY WHITE
Barry White's Greatest Hits Vol. 2
1977
UK POLYDOR 822783-2
The Collection *1988*
UK: MERCURY 834790 2
Greatest Hits *1975*
UK: POLYDOR 822782-2
The Right Night And Barry White
1987
UK: A&M CDA5154

KARYN WHITE
Karyn White *1989*
UK: WARNER BROS 925637 2
Ritual Of Love *1991*
UK: WARNER BROS 7599263202
US: WARNER BROS 263202-2

DENIECE WILLIAMS
This Is Niecey *1977*
US: COLUMBIA CK34242

BILL WITHERS
Greatest Hits *1988*
UK: COLUMBIA CD32343
The Sound Of Soul (Bill Withers)
1980
UK: CASTLE BLATCD 13

Watching You Watching Me *1985*
JAPAN: SONY SRCS 6132

BOBBY WOMACK
Facts Of Life
1973
UK: UNITED ARTISTS CDCHARLY157
The Poet *1982*
UK: BEVERLY GLEN BGCD10000
The Poet II *1984*
UK: MOTOWN BGD10003
So Many Rivers
1985
UK: MCA DMCF3282/L1894
The Very Best of Bobby Womack
1991
UK: MCI MCCD018

WOMACK AND WOMACK
Conscience
1988
UK: 4TH & BROADWAY BRCD519
US: 4TH & BROADWAY CID1189
Love Wars *1984*
UK: ELEKTRA 9603127
US: ELEKTRA 960293-2
Radio M.U.S.C. Man
1985
UK: ELEKTRA K9604062

STEVIE WONDER
Characters
1987
UK: MOTOWN ZD72001
US: MOTOWN MOTD 6248

Essential Stevie Wonder
1987
UK: MOTOWN ZD72585
US: MOTOWN WD72585
Fulfillingness' First Finale
1974
UK: MOTOWN WD72607
US: MOTOWN MOTD 332
Greatest Hits Vol. 2
1972
UK: MOTOWN WD72669
US: MOTOWN MOTD 313
Hotter Than July
1980
UK: MOTOWN ZD72015
US: MOTOWN MOTD 9064
In Square Circle
1985
UK: MOTOWN ZD72005
US: MOTOWN MOTD 6134
Innervisions *1973*
UK: MOTOWN ZD72012
US: MOTOWN MOTD 326
Journey Through The Secret Life Of Plants *1979*
UK: MOTOWN ZD72145
US: MOTOWN MOSD 6291
Jungle Fever *1991*
UK: MOTOWN ZD72750
US: MOTOWN MOSD 6291
Little Stevie Wonder/12 Year Old Genius
1963
US: TAMLA MOTD 5131
Love Songs—16 Classic Hits
1984
UK: MOTOWN WD72389
US: MOTOWN MOTD 9050

Music Of My Mind
1972
UK: TAMLA WD72604
US: MOTOWN MOTD 314
My Cherie Amour
1969
UK: MOTOWN WD72077
US: MOTOWN MOTD 5179
Original Musiquarium
1982
UK: MOTOWN ZD72225
Signed Sealed And Delivered *1970*
UK: TAMLA WD72186
US: MOTOWN MOTD 5176
Songs In The Key Of Life
1976
UK: MOTOWN ZD72131
US: MOTOWN MOTD 2-340
Stevie Wonder's Greatest Hits
1968
UK: MOTOWN WD72668
US: MOTOWN MOTD 282
Talking Book
1973
UK: MOTOWN ZD72011
US: MOTOWN MOTD 319
Up-Tight Everything's Alright
1966
US: TAMLA 3746351832
Woman In Red *1984*
UK: MOTOWN WD72609

index

Page numbers in italics refer to captions to illustrations

acknowledgements

Photographs reproduced by kind permission of London Features
International/Juliette Avis, Juanita Cole, Paul Cox, Nick Elgar, Martin
Esseveld, Gie Knaeps, Michel Linssen, Ilpo Musto, Mike Prior, Epet
Roberts, Govert De Roos, George De Sota and Ron Wolfson; Rex
Features/Peter Brooker, Jan Meyer and Jerry Wachter.

Front jacket: Pictorial Press/Keuntje.
Back jacket from left to right: Rex Features, Retna/Jay Blakesberg,
Pictorial Press, Rex Features, Retna/M. Putland.